Teaching at Home

also by Olga Holland

The Dragons of Autism
Autism as a Source of Wisdom
ISBN 1 84310 741 4

of related interest

Homeschooling the Child with Asperger Syndrome
Real Help for Parents Anywhere and On Any Budget
Lise Pyles
ISBN 1 84310 761 9

Home Educating Our Autistic Spectrum Children
Paths are Made by Walking
Edited by Terri Dowty and Kitt Cowlishaw
ISBN 1 84310 037 1

Choosing Home
Deciding to Homeschool with Asperger's Syndrome
Martha Kennedy Hartnett
Foreword by Stephen Shore
ISBN 1 84310 763 5

Asperger's Syndrome
A Guide for Parents and Professionals
Tony Attwood
Foreword by Lorna Wing
ISBN 1 85302 577 1

Teaching at Home

A New Approach to Tutoring Children with Autism and Asperger Syndrome

Olga Holland

Jessica Kingsley Publishers
London and Philadelphia

Illustrations and poems by Billy Holland

First published in 2005
by Jessica Kingsley Publishers
116 Pentonville Road
London N1 9JB, UK
and
400 Market Street, Suite 400
Philadelphia, PA 19106, USA

www.jkp.com

Library of Congress Cataloging in Publication Data
Holland, Olga, 1957-
  Teaching at home : a new approach to tutoring children with autism and Asperger syndrome / Olga Holland.
    p. cm.
  ISBN-13: 978-1-84310-787-3 (pbk.)
  ISBN-10: 1-84310-787-2 (pbk.)
  1. Autistic children—Education. 2. Home schooling. 3. Asperger's syndrome. I. Title.
  LC4717.5.H65 2005
  371.94—dc22

                                                        2005003014

British Library Cataloguing in Publication Data
A CIP catalogue record for this book is available from the British Library

ISBN-13: 978 1 84310 787 3
ISBN-10: 1 84310 787 2

Printed and Bound in Great Britain by
Athenaeum Press, Gateshead, Tyne and Wear

Contents

Part III A Teacher's Strategies

Part IV Afterthoughts and Milestones

Introduction

A few words about the structure of this book. The chapters in Part I are about us – about Billy and his troubles as an autistic child, and about my troubles as his parent. I also talk about facing the dilemma – "To teach or not to teach" – and about how I came to choose "To teach!"

Part II contains what I call, to myself, the "attention-chasing" chapters. The challenge of tutoring a child with autism or Asperger Syndrome is to win over the child's inner world, where his attention can be trapped for hours at a time. In Part II I talk about this war for attention, about ways to drag the child's attention away from the beauty of his inner world and into the emptiness of a white page in front of him which he is to fill with figures that are meaningless to him.

I've tried these attention-chasing techniques on many children, including my typical daughter. They work on almost everyone, although it's much harder to chase the attention of a child with low-functioning autism than of a child with high-functioning autism or Asperger Syndrome.

In Part III of the book, I describe the practical exercises and learning strategies that were of great help in teaching Billy. To me, all the techniques I write about were indispensable. They are easy to use one-on-one, but some of them, such as teaching words by singing them out loud, would be hard to apply in a classroom setting. When I started teaching Billy difficult words like "subtraction" it was much easier for him to sing them than to say them. But after learning to sing them, he could say them as well.

I reserved the last part of the book for sharing some odd thoughts and for outlining Billy's progress in our home school.

I truly hope to inspire you to work with your child. It doesn't have to be full time; even 30 minutes a day can lead to progress. I wish you luck.

Prologue

When I was little, my nanny told me a story.

A man dies and, to his good fortune, goes to Heaven. He finds Heaven full of people, all of them sitting at tables loaded with delightful foods. They are wonderfully merry as they enjoy Heaven's abundance.

But when he asks where he should sit, an angel directs the man to an empty table. Indignant, the man appeals to God: "God, this is not fair. Why do these people have so much, and I have nothing?"

"Because," God answers, "each of them has what he or she has given to others while on Earth. But you, while on Earth, gave to no one. Nothing given, nothing gained. As your giving hand was empty on Earth, so your table is empty in Heaven."

"O, God!" the man cries, "Forgive me! Please, give me another chance! Let me go back to the Earth and change my ways!"

"All right," God says, "I'll give you another chance." And the man finds himself back on Earth.

The man becomes agitated and busy. He bakes loaf after loaf of good bread and fills a huge sack with the loaves. Then he loads the heavy sack onto his back and heads back to Heaven. But on his way, trudging on a dirt road, he slips. One loaf slides from the sack on his back and falls into the dirt. The man turns back after the fallen loaf, but then, seeing how dirty it is, leaves it there and goes on. A while later, a hungry vagabond beggar walks by. He sees the bread in the dirt and grabs it. He eats it, feeling grateful to the person who left it there.

Back in Heaven he turns in the bread to the receiving angel and goes to his table. In the middle of the table he finds one single loaf of bread. It is the fallen loaf, full of dirt.

When my time comes, and I find myself, I hope, in Heaven, on my table maybe I will find my books, this one and my first book, *The Dragons of Autism*. They are my gift to others. The books are about my autistic boy, Billy, and how he changed our lives. The first tells how we learned to direct Billy's emotions. The second is about directing Billy's mind.

Truly, children change the lives of their parents. The lives of the parents of autistic children change even more. For a long time, I resisted the impositions of a reality that had autism in it. I tried to hold on to some "life of my own." That didn't work. Resistance, in itself, was hard. And there was no "life of my own" anyway. And then I let Billy's autism be a "life of my own." Instead of resisting life with autism, I made myself a part of it.

Evolution teaches us not to resist new conditions, but to adapt to them. Life with autism, as compared to a typical life, is like life in Siberia compared to life in San Diego. In a life with storms and snow, resistance is not the answer. The answer is learning to keep warm.

I'm still in the process of adapting to life with autism. As I learn more about this environment, I also gain new skills and master the craft of managing it.

This book is about our home school – The Aristotle School for the Bright and Gifted. It's about adapting to the demands of Billy's atypical mind. It's about how I trusted that Billy was bright and gifted, and worked hard to make sure that he is educated too.

I hope this book will inspire other parents to adapt and grow in new environments: to grow wings, to learn to shed skins, to swim in rough waters, or to climb high rocks. Whatever it takes. The children will respond – perhaps each in a special way, some sooner than others. But they will respond, if we keep our faith strong – so strong that God will gasp in awe and give us a helping hand.

PART I

The Journey to the Aristotle School

My name is Billy.

Son of Olga and Bill

Who needs love, T-V, and tag.

Who fears dark, dark shapes, and heights.

I am a kid who loves my mom.

I always wash my face.

I move like waves.

I read fantasy.

I never murder.

No one knows I have secret thoughts.

I am a good person

I bring magic.

Chapter 1

Billy grows up

Our family is of an average size – a father, a mother, a firstborn girl, and a second child, joining the Earth 22 months after the girl, a boy.

The girl, born in 1991, was named Francesca. Her life journey unfolded easily. It followed, with magical accuracy, a predictable path that fitted perfectly into the human world. We took that for granted because we thought that's how childhood was supposed to be. She set out to be what a child should be – a permanent source of joy to her parents.

The boy, born in 1993, was named William. The parents called him, at various times, Baby Bill, Little Bill and Bilchick (based on the way names of endearment are formed in Russian). Eventually, at the boy's insistence, the family and everyone else settled for calling him Billy.

Billy's life journey has not been anything like "That's how it's supposed to be." There is no one-sentence summary of Billy's life journey. We knew that there was *something* different about Billy very soon after his arrival. As a baby, he could not be made to smile. His first smile didn't appear until he was six months old. This was different from our daughter and from other babies we knew, but it did not worry us. Physically, he developed very well. He was healthy and strong. We saw our doctor for checkups and vaccines. The doctor admired Billy's development and encouraged Mom to "keep on doing whatever she is doing."

I was born in Mount Pleasants in New York State, on August 31 1993.

Billy

At age two Billy was not talking, and he interacted little with other children. The doctor saw no reason to worry. However, a visiting friend who happened to be a specialist in child development suggested that there *were* reasons to worry, and she recommended that we consult an "early intervention" facility. We did that. Billy got a label – "language development delay" – and was assigned 45 minutes of therapy once a week.

At age three Billy was saying about 20 single words, to name such things as juice or milk, but it was obvious that he had no command of language as a tool for communication. It also became apparent that his behavior was not typical of children of his age. By the time children reach three years of age, they are commonly expected:

- to look to adults for directions
- to make eye contact
- to be happy when they have companionship
- to be grumpy only rarely, mostly at times of discomfort
- to have temper tantrums only at times of severe discomfort
- to show fear in some circumstances
- to obey their parents' rules of the house
- to want to please their parents, at least for the sake of a reward.

Billy did not do what children are supposed to do. Billy got up every morning with an agenda; he had an agenda of his own pretty much at all other times of the day as well. He did not look to adults for directions. He followed his own directions, and he really wanted adults to follow his directions as well. When they didn't he was displeased, which led, as you might imagine, to conflicts.

At about two we realized that Billy avoided looking into anyone's eyes. That definitely raised our awareness of the importance of eye contact for communication between humans. It also became apparent that Billy was not quite grasping the rules for good companionship. Whether in the company of adults or children, he managed in no time to annoy everyone around him.

A "happy child" Billy was not. He was grumpy; grumpy because of one discomfort or another. And he had a remarkable ability to find discomforts. It seemed that for Billy the mere process of living was a continuous discomfort. Almost everything seemed to be a potential irritant.

Whether he was going to bed or getting out of bed, getting into a bath or getting out of it, getting into the car or getting out of it, sitting down to eat or finishing eating, for Billy simple functions of life never just started and finished. Starting any daily routine became a transition (i.e., a time of severe discomfort), and so did completing the routine. After age two, Billy started reacting to more and more transitions with tantrums – emotional reactions bordering, at their height, on hysterical, uncontrollable protests against reality.

It was impossible to intimidate Billy. Billy's body didn't manufacture an intimidation chemical, and the lack of it proved to be more than just inconvenient. Like it or not, intimidation is a big part of bringing up most children. Parents communicate fear of heights, fear of fire, fear of electrical outlets, fear of knives and so on. However, if a child has no fear – has no idea what fear is – there's really nothing to stop him from doing whatever he wants. There are only two brain functions that ultimately control a social order: reason and fear. A one-year old is not subject to reason. If he has no fear either, it means trouble.

For a long time, the only way we could keep Billy out of danger was to grab him and remove him physically. Only at about age six did Billy start becoming aware of the dangers of the world. The first time he ever showed any sense of danger was at the seashore, on a day with rough waves, when Billy asked if it was all right for him to go into the water. Before that, he'd always just rush into the waves and let us worry about his safety. Later on, when he was seven and had quite a bit of English at his command, I discovered that I could reason at last with him as well.

Billy did not know how to obey. Non-obedience was his second skin. In fact it served to his advantage to such a degree that it made me wonder why on earth most children go on obeying their parents.

And Billy did not care about pleasing anybody in this world. If he didn't care to say a new word, he wouldn't say it. He wouldn't say it for candy. He wouldn't say it for a toy, not even if it was a dragon. He didn't even look at you. He wasn't concerned in the least whether your face showed gladness or sorrow; he didn't notice your face. Oblivious to states of minds around him, he was oblivious to the fact that he could influence them.

Billy did not participate in the game of pleasing people and being praised for it. For a long time he was not even aware of the game. He was in his own world. It would be hard to make an accountant out of a person who is not aware of the game of numbers in math. It's hard to raise a socially compatible human out of a child who is not aware of the game of emotions in our lives.

Chapter 2

Face to face with autism

When Billy was four we learned that he was autistic. We were somewhat relieved. Not because the word autistic inspired optimism, but because we were not alone in the wilderness anymore. There was somebody out there who knew, first hand, what we were going through. There were people who could understand and support.

Billy joined a special education class in the San Diego school district. At first we didn't realize how lucky we were. His first teacher, Theresa, was a woman with great experience in special education. More importantly she was (and is) blessed with an uncommon talent for seeing, in every child who joins her class, not a problem, but a way to let a miracle happen. And she has angelic patience. She teaches her students as if she's got plenty of time. Would you dream of going into a special education class to relax? I didn't before I met Theresa, but I do go to Theresa's class to relax. As I watch her directing a dozen or fourteen children, each of them highly atypical, I gain faith that God really can act through some of us. For nothing earthly can explain the generosity of her heart.

We brought to Theresa an aggressive, unmanageable boy, age four. He didn't talk, he wasn't potty trained and he would bite when things didn't go right. Three months into the school year, Theresa gave us her verdict: "Oh, school's hard for him, but he'll be much better in college." Seeing our eyebrows rising above our foreheads, she added, firmly and gently, "Oh yes, he *will* go to college." At the time, he wasn't even out of diapers. I cannot overstate the importance of having someone give us a vision beyond those diapers.

In Theresa's hands Billy went from being just a problem to being a problem who had at least one talent. She was the first to utilize Billy's talent for drama. She used it to get him to participate in activities which were orchestrated by someone other than himself. Theresa also discovered in Billy the capacity for logical thinking. And she succeeded in making him learn words.

The year in Theresa's class gave us tremendous hope for Billy's development. We relaxed. We were grateful to the San Diego school system, and we were looking forward to having our child trained in the same manner for years to come. It appeared, though, that our relaxation was premature. The San Diego school district indeed has an admirable special education department. Many accomplished specialists work in it, and they spare no effort to make a difference. But they can do only what they can do. They can provide a classroom with a trained teacher for every child. They can't provide Theresa for every child.

For the next two years, in kindergarten and in the first grade, Billy's progress could not compare to what he had done in Theresa's class. Gradually, I grew more restless. As time went on, it became more and more obvious how much Billy was lagging behind.

Six weeks into his second grade, I withdrew Billy from the school system and started teaching him at home. We opened our own school.

write each word 2 times.
Read all of them outloud.

1.	heel	heel	heel
2.	heat	heat	heat
3.	heap	heap	heap
4.	it seems	it seems	it seems
5.	cute seal	cute seal	cute seal
6.	little seed	little seed	little seed
7.	I seek	I seek	I seek
8.	green leaves	green leaves	green leaves
9.	gray sheep	gray sheep	gray sheep
10.	marble beads	marble beads	marble beads

Chapter 3

Making the decision

When Billy finished first grade, I was not a happy person. In his special education class he wasn't asked to take any tests. He didn't know how to take one. And I knew that if he did take a test, he wouldn't score anywhere close to first grade level. His social progress was negative: he had learned new ways of interacting with people, but he seemed to learn mostly ways which were not good.

So I organized a summer school for Billy. That summer was a trial for both of us, but we endured it and came to some valuable conclusions. Number one, the good one, was that Billy was capable of learning. Number two was that for him it was possible to learn only on a one-to-one basis, which meant that if we wanted him to gain academically, there was no point in sending him back to a special education class. Even though Billy had a full-time assistant, a special education class with eight to twelve special children is a busy place. I knew how easy it was for Billy's mind to be distracted from learning. My one-to-one approach meant, in fact, one teacher, one student, and nobody else.

The school district had no way to accommmodate an individual space with an individual teacher for a single child. The one-on-one arrangements which I have seen in special education classes consist of a desk with a

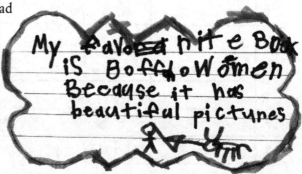

My favourite Book is Boffalo Women Because it has beautiful pictures

screen blocking all views. This definitely helps somewhat. It blocks visual distractions, but it doesn't block the auditory distractions, and they too can be powerful. Auditory distractions could certainly overpower Billy. During that summer, he would often lose track of what we were doing at the sound of an airplane or the chirp of a bird.

But even such an arrangement – blocked desks for single students – was available only in classes for children with problems more severe than Billy's. I didn't think it was a good idea to have him there. The next best thing the district could offer was a class of 12 children in which the children studied with different teachers, three students to one teacher. The classroom was divided into sections, and the four teachers taught their groups in separate corners.

We observed that classroom, and we liked it. The teachers seemed able to control their three-student groups. The classroom was equipped with visual aids, with computers. So we went for it.

September came. Billy started at the school. He liked it. Early every morning he got on the school bus and off he went. When he came home in the late afternoon, he was happy. When asked how his day was, he said "Good." I could have relaxed, in principle, but by then Billy's contentedness wasn't enough for me. He had been contented at school the two years before, too. Now I needed to know not just that he was content, but that he was learning as well.

At the end of his second week, I went to check what was going on in his school. I wanted to talk with the teacher about homework, it bothered me that Billy wasn't bringing any home. I came to school and asked permission to observe. The first thing I observed was that Billy was in the wrong classroom. He was in a class for children with severe deficiencies. There were six other children in the class, and five aides. The other children had no command of language. Because of that, the classwork was unstructured. Practically every child needed customized intervention, and many different things were happening at the same time in the room. Billy liked it all. He thought it was great fun.

I went to the school office to inquire. His placement appeared to be the result of a typing mistake. The typist had put Billy's name in the wrong place, and as a result he had been sent to the wrong class. He was immediately transferred to the class where he was supposed to be. I know mistakes happen. I also know that there are parents who are too busy to go to schools. They see the child at home after work, and if the child says that he had a good, fun day, the parents are satisfied. Things are going well. It ain't necessarily so.

With Billy now in the right class, I decided to make sure that I knew for myself what was happening in his day, so I began going to his school early in the morning, before classes started. Before class, children got off their buses and played in the playground. Depending on the time the bus arrived, this playtime lasted 10 or 15 minutes. I observed those 15 minutes. The atmosphere during playtime was rough and noisy. At the end of it, Billy was agitated and over-stimulated. When the bell rang, all the children were supposed to line up in the rows assigned for their different classes. Billy had trouble standing in a line. He had trouble just standing still. He pushed the children in front of him and those behind him. He continued to make the noises which he had been making on the playground. Many other children did the same.

As a result of this observation, I decided to drive Billy to school myself and to set up a calm transition from home to school. On the way to school, I played classical music on the car stereo, something gentle and soothing. I took a blanket with me: the mornings were chilly, and Billy didn't like cold. I took Billy's favorite snack. When we arrived at school, I coaxed him into sitting on a bench to have a snack and listen to me read a story. I told him that as soon as he finished his snack he could go and join the children in the playground if he wanted. But by the time he finished his snack, I was well into the story, and he was curious to know what came next. I went on to drive him to school every morning. It quickly became our ritual. By the time the bell rang, Billy was as peaceful as could be. He was doing better in line; he was less agitated.

Soon after I started keeping Billy company, I noticed that two boys from his class would come close and stand behind me as I read. It took them a week until, step by step, they finally sat with us on the bench. I was happy to have them. There were two problems: we had to share our snack, and the blanket was too small to wrap everybody in. By the end of the second week into the ritual, we had four boys joining us.

I started having an urge to organize a campaign, to find volunteers who would agree to come in the mornings to read and comfort children, and maybe to come at lunchtime, too. I could see how lost many of the children seemed, getting off the bus and onto the odd, noisy, overpopulated school grounds. I didn't follow up on my urge. I had to concentrate on taking care of Billy's needs, because that was in itself a full-time campaign.

I began observing Billy in his class. He was manageable in a group of three students. But now that you have an idea what kind of person I am, you may guess that there's going to be a *but* and you're right. There was a "but". Actually, there were several "buts". Among them – but the children in class moved from one section to another, changing desks and teachers. Billy is autistic. He performs best within a regime of repetitive, similar procedures and spaces. Every change requires adjustment time and adjustment energy. I wished that Billy's energy could be saved for learning. I wished he had a desk with his name on it, as a secure anchor in space. I wished he had only one teacher working with him. After our summer class, I knew how difficult it was to discover ways in which Billy could learn one thing or another. Knowledge of Billy's ways had to be cumulative knowledge, collected with great care. Teachers who had to keep switching students couldn't collect enough of it.

I tried to have regular meetings with Billy's teachers so that I'd be well informed about his performance in the class, in order to support it at home. This didn't work out. His teachers didn't have time for discussions on a regular basis. I felt like a beggar who could spot an unspoken "No Soliciting" sign written in the teacher's mind.

Again, it would have been easy just let go of all this. The other children's parents didn't seem to be bothered by these details. But I couldn't let go. From what I knew about autism, one thing was clear: the later intervention starts, the harder it is to get significant results. I had had the benefit of seeing Billy in Theresa's class, where the intervention was highly customized and every child was pushed to make progress.

Billy was already seven. Time was pressing. For two years his education had taken an easy, unburdened course, but now I felt these had been two years of lost opportunities. He was unburdened by an education. I felt that the way he was being taught didn't make use of his potential. Frustrated mom that I was, fearing the thought of raising a boy who might not be able to function independently in the future, I couldn't help but notice all the "buts".

What could the school system do to help me? Not much more than it was already doing. I was aching for a personal approach to my boy's education, but asking for that would have been like asking for a personal menu for him at school lunchtime. There wasn't one. If I wanted my child to have a personal menu, I had to provide it myself, whether for food or education. So I made the decision to withdraw Billy from school and teach him myself.

When I told my husband, Bill, of my proposal to teach Billy, he did not share my enthusiasm. Billy's time in school was a much needed break for both of us. Twenty-four consecutive hours with an autistic child are about twenty too many. I know Bill worried about me. He didn't want me to have an emotional breakdown down further down the road. He worried about Billy too. After all, I was proposing to take Billy away not only from an unsatisfactory education, but also from other children. He would miss them. And what if I couldn't manage? What would we do with Billy then? The truth was that the education offered by the school was a very, very good alternative to nothing. Why destroy that alternative and venture into an unknown – an unknown with an unknown probability of failure.

Theresa was not excited about my decision either, and for the same reasons. Everyone needs a break from an autistic child. As Theresa says, "A parent should have a chance to say 'goodbye' to an autistic child. Because if you don't have a chance to say 'goodbye',' then it's always 'hello', 'hello', 'hello'. And there is no timeout for a reality check."

Once Bill and Theresa saw that describing the downside didn't shake my determination, they both set out to help me. Theresa was ready to share her experience with me. Bill helped with the paperwork for the home school and settled matters with the district. As for me, I tried hard not think about all the possible downsides. I was so aware of them. Dwelling on them was utterly unconstructive and only made me sad and weighed me down emotionally. So I tried to concentrate on a positive vision. In that vision, Billy liked my school. In that vision, he enjoyed learning, and learning was easy. In that vision, I liked teaching and did it well. And there was happiness and laughter in our school. To make sure that I would have a tangible reflection for my vision, I made a sign for our school. It said "Aristotle School for the Bright and Gifted."

Chapter 4

The deal with the district

In some special education classes, children are sent for part of the day to an "inclusion program" in a regular class. The child is sent for only a little time at first, and the time is gradually increased according to his progress in the class. When Billy was in kindergarten he was in a school which had a very strong inclusion program, and he went to a regular class for 30 minutes to an hour at a time. His assistant went with him. Billy did well in the regular class.

I was in favor of continuing Billy's inclusion program. I believed that he benefited tremendously from spending time among typical children. Unfortunately a full-time assignment to a special education class leaves a special child little room to gain an understanding about the routine and demands of a typical class.

Homeschooling, in that way, is somewhat like special education, but homeschooling did not have to conflict with an inclusion program. After a good deal of thought, I came up with a simple plan. In the morning, from 9:00am to noon Billy would study at home, in the Aristotle School. After lunch he would join a regular class, with an assistant, for the rest of the day.

We approached the school district with our request for this combination of homeschooling with an inclusion program. We were very

I hate being alone.
I hate eating fish and rice.

fortunate to find in our local elementary school an understanding principal who fully supported our request. So Billy was going to start his inclusion in Loma Portal Elementary. Finding an assistant for him promised to be problematic. We needed an aide for only two and a half hours daily, four days a week (the school had Thursday afternoons off). It wouldn't be easy to find a competent person for so little time so until we could find someone to work with Billy, I was allowed to assist him in the classroom. So we were set. Billy was in the second grade and he was assigned to a second grade taught by a lovely and very welcoming teacher.

As for the curriculum at home, I was left to myself. The homeschooling office of the district had no experience with autistic children and could offer little to assist me. To me, that didn't matter. Although Billy was officially a second grader, he knew less than a good graduate of a kindergarten class. So my curriculum was simple – start with the first grade. If we succeeded in moving at a typical pace and covered the whole first grade curriculum in our homeschooling year, we'd be in good shape.

In mid-October Billy started learning the basics of knowledge in the Aristotle School, and shortly after that we joined the second grade at Loma Portal for the afternoon program. The children in the second grade class were nice to Billy. The teacher was very nice to Billy. But inclusion in the second grade didn't work. Billy's acquired knowledge and his vocabulary were not sufficient to keep him involved in the class. Whether it was math, science, or reading, Billy got bored because he couldn't keep up with what was going on. And a bored Billy is trouble.

When Billy is bored, he doesn't sit and gaze absentmindedly out a window. When Billy is bored, he strives to do something that is not boring. Like sliding off the chair, making faces at other children, exploring the classroom or making noises. My assisting with Billy in his inclusion program turned into a test of endurance. I could be firm and impose discipline on him, but disciplining Billy is hard and it takes undivided effort. If I had to worry about being quiet and not disrupting the class, I couldn't do it.

We had to abandon our second grade inclusion program. After a while I talked to the principal of the school. I asked if we could put Billy back one year and start him, officially, as a first grader. Judged by his social and academic skills, certainly he was more a first grader than a second, and his curriculum in our home school was a first grade curriculum as well.

The principal agreed that our request made sense. Billy was assigned to a first grade class for his afternoons. Billy didn't actually start going to the first grade class at the public school until March though, when the school finally found an aide for him. Until then, he studied at home for the whole day.

Billy's aide was Justin, a student at a local college. He had no experience in special education. However, his kindness and desire to learn made up for that. Justin stayed with Billy through the rest of his first grade and then returned in the fall to assist him in the second grade. He became a good friend to Billy. This time, inclusion went very well. Billy loved the reading circle; he could understand and process the stories very well. He could do all the math assignments. He loved the art projects.

The combination of homeschooling plus inclusion in a regular class worked well for Billy. His teachers in both first grade and second grade noticed gradual progress in his ability to function in the classroom. He learned to raise his hand before asking a question. He learned that when bored, he should walk quietly to the book baskets, choose a book, return to his chair and read to himself. He learned names of the children and the games they liked to play.

Once in a while I would ask Billy if he was ready to give up "Momma's school" and go study with the children full-time. For a long time Billy's answer was, "No, Mom. Your school makes me smart. I learn stuff with you, and then I can go and be smart at school with the kids." Only by the end of our second year of homeschooling was he finally ready for full-time inclusion. Then he told me, "I think I'd like to be in the kids' school all the time now, Mom."

Chapter 5

Setting up a school at home

Of course, naming our school after Aristotle wasn't a panacea against its failure. In planning our homeschooling venture, I tried to sort out what was up to me and what would have to be left for a higher interference. Certainly, I had sanguine expectations for deific assistance in my teaching. But I also knew that there was a truth in the Russian saying that "Water doesn't run under a resting stone", which is an equivalent to "No pain, no gain". And where could the pain possibly come from?

1. Billy refuses to acknowledge me as teacher and tries to coax me into being Mom.

2. Billy has a hard time making the transition from home as home to home as school.

3. Billy is distracted by things at home such as toys, television, food, the backyard swing, etc.

4. Being a homeschool teacher takes perseverance. A *lot* of perseverance. I have some perseverance. Will it be enough?

What could I do to make some gain in spite of these pains?

Being a teacher, and not just Mom

First, I needed to look like a teacher. This meant that I was going to dress up for Billy's home school just as if I were teaching at the University of California – hair, make-up, earrings and all.

At the time our first child arrived, my husband and I were living on the twenty-first floor of a building on Roosevelt Island, in the middle of the East

River, next to Manhattan. It was a good living. New York is great place for one who likes to discover things anew.

And then we moved. Driven by greed for extra rooms, we left the city. The idea of having a huge house in Connecticut for no more than we paid for our three rooms in the city was irresistible. We planned to move right before Billy was born. As it turned out, we moved exactly as Billy was being born. In our new (old) house, there was a room for Francesca, a room for the new baby, a room for sewing, a room for guests, a living room, a dining room, and more. If space was to make me happy, I was in for a lot of happiness. Man proposes, God disposes. We lived in suburban Connecticut for three years. To me, they were long, long years. The morning train took Bill to his Manhattan office. I was left behind to join the invisible army of suburban mothers. I bought sweats to fit in. But, as I was to learn, clothes have a power of their own. My new relaxed attire affected my mind. Losing the competitive drive to show off to the city, I developed a sweats mentality.

Ultimately, I could not stomach belonging to an invisible army; but for a while I endured. The three years in Connecticut I call my three years of exile. Freedom came when we moved back to the city. I took my sweats to a thrift shop, and in my closet I hung new, sharp city clothes. My mind, happily, put on a sharpness of its own. So when I ventured into teaching Billy, I knew better than to sport pajama-like attire. I had first-hand experience of the connection between suitable attire and a suitable mind.

At the beginning of our homeschooling, Billy tried to take advantage of our close relationship, seeking affection or trying to curl up in my lap for comfort. Clad in my professional garb, it was easy enough for me to settle things. Using a suitably professional voice, I pointed out to Billy the distribution of our tasks. "Excuse me Billy. We are in school now, and I'm the teacher. You are the student. When we're finished, I'll go back to being a mom, and you can be my little boy. But not yet."

The transition from home to school

Home has a very specific energy. Usually it's a relaxed energy, one of good meals, sweet naps, family time. When a child goes to school outside the home, all the surroundings support a shift into a working mood. The classes, the teachers and the backpacks all help children to orient their minds toward school. At home it was just Billy and me. Somehow we needed to move from a cuddly morning into the collectedness of mind that is essential for learning. Help came from creating a ritual.

Creating a ritual is like making a quilt. When you make a quilt, for a while the work is monotonous and repetitive. Whether the quilt has 20 blocks or 40, each one has to be started, finished, put aside; then another is made. Only when all the blocks are finished can there be a transition to the next step putting all the blocks together. Then, for the first time we first see how, united, they interlock magically into the geometry of a new quilt. Then the quilt is sewn together, secured by tiny stitches for long use. But after all that work, there's going to be a quilt. It will be filled with comfort, warmth and protection.

A new ritual, in the beginning, takes a lot of hard repetitive work. Before it can be a ritual, it must be a daily task. Every day it must be started anew from the beginning and taken every day to completion, like the blocks of a quilt. It may take 20 or 40 days, or more, until all of the efforts connect, magically, into the pattern of a new ritual. Then still more effort will be needed to secure that pattern for long use. But after all that work, there's going to be a ritual. It will have a message of its own, and it will be comforting when it can be jumped into effortlessly.

Our morning ritual was tightly scheduled. We took Francesca to school at 8:40 am. From there we drove to the shore to wave at the ships slipping in and out of San Diego Bay. We spent only about ten minutes there, but those minutes were precious. The smell of the ocean, the seagulls, the occasional seals all took us away from the cuddly morning at home. Braced by the salt breeze, we returned home as if from a long trip. And we didn't return home to home, we returned home to school. Billy was given 15 minutes of free time, and at 9:15 he was to be at Aristotle School for the first class. Meanwhile, I'd slip into my teacher role. I talked to Billy like a teacher, I walked like a teacher, I even squinted my eyes a little, just to add to my character.

It took less than 20 days for the ritual to become the magic-worker it needed to be. In the beginning, Billy would question the need for schooling, or he'd try to negotiate more time at the sea or more free time. But little by little the questioning attitude ceased, borne away by the comfort of the new ritual.

In time Billy learned to slip effortlessly into the self-regulating ritual. Each morning he said hello and goodbye to the sea, used his free time to browse through a book or play outside, and was ready, when the ring of my voice announced the start of school, to proceed with learning.

Distraction

To free Billy from the distractions of home, I needed to create a feng shui version of a home school – a place pleasant and inviting, yet intellectually stimulating. I was fortunate that we had a garage separate from our house. It was a hillside garage and under it, with its own entrance on the downhill side, was a games room that I had converted into my sewing room. I had dedicated it to quilting. Now the hobby I had acquired in America and learned to love would have to wait for other times. I squeezed my sewing things into a small part of the room. The freed space became the Aristotle School for the Bright and Gifted.

I bought few new things for our school. A small but perfectly usable writing board for the wall came from Costco. Two small stools and two small floor shelves came from Ikea. I found a bookshelf in a neighborhood thrift shop. We had an extra desk and a chair. A beige carpet I grabbed at Pic' n' Save. I also scouted our local educational supply stores and came home with a few lovely posters depicting our solar system, the rules for using short and long vowels, and the circulation of water on Earth.

On the Saturday before our first week of school, I hurried to the Russian Orthodox Church in San Diego and bought two icons; one of Mother Mary and the other of Nicolas the Miracle-Maker. I hung them on the wall and asked them to be our silent witnesses and supporters.

My efforts paid off. On Monday morning Billy went into the classroom and loved it. He wanted to stay in it. The space invited him and puzzled him. I could see wonder in his eyes, I could see expectations. It was up to me to fulfill them.

Perseverance

Willpower works like singing. Good country singing may not bring success at the opera. In the past, I'd had the willpower to walk barefoot in the snow, to fast, to keep a secret, to be up at sunrise. That kind of power, though, was not enough to sustain the role of teacher of an autistic child in a home school. When Billy's mind did not cooperate in class, I became turbulent and restless, filled with revolt and helplessness. I gazed at the icons of Mother Mary and Nicolas the Miracle-Maker, hoping against hope not to sound and not to look the way I felt.

If I was to be a good teacher for Billy, I needed help. I set about learning self-control. Eventually I put together a set of self-relaxation exercises along with some self-hypnosis and energy therapy. These helped tremendously. They made me an armed soldier, they became my ammunition on the field of teaching. My ammunition included:

- understanding the roots of my emotional responses
- finding ways to respond from reason rather than from emotion
- starting each day with a set of exercises which set an emotional balance for the day
- understanding the roots of Billy's emotional responses and learning to help him find his own emotional balance.

But no ammunition is a substitute for strength of spirit. Real patience and perseverance come when our spirit approves of our task. Before I could learn to let go of stress and just wait, I had to feel that teaching Billy was not merely my choice; it was more than my choice. Before I could acquire the will to teach Billy forcefully yet gently and without expectations, I had to sense that I was fulfilling the will of the spirit.

A Tree Story

There was a There was a boy and his nam was Tom. In his backyard there was a tree. One day the boy saw that the leves noon the tree are looking ill. The boy found a tree doctor. the tree doctor sprayed the tree with medicine and the tree was saved.

Chapter 6

Homework

From the beginning of his homeschooling, I gave Billy a minimum of one hour of homework. In the second grade his homework went to an average of two hours a day – an hour and a half from me and a half hour from the public school. I've been told that this is a lot, that in a typical class children do much less. True. However, a child with scoliosis may be prescribed a strenuous regimen of exercises to straighten the spine. Nobody would question the wisdom of this, even though a typical child doesn't need them. To me it seemed quite logical to have a strenuous regimen of mental exercises to strengthen a mind that had developed slowly.

At first Billy did learn slowly. He had difficulties with comprehension. To me that meant that we had to work much harder with him than we ever did with our daughter Francesca, to whom learning was an open field. Billy had homework four days a week – no homework on Fridays or weekends. His schedule worked like this. On Mondays, we'd take the homework package that came from Loma Portal. It was the same package that was given to the other children in his inclusion class; but the others had time until Friday to finish it. We made Billy do that homework on Monday. On Tuesday, Wednesday and Thursday he had the Aristotle School's homework.

"How come", Billy asked me, "I get so much homework, and the other kids don't?" I told him that the other kids go to only one school, so they get one homework. He goes to two schools, so he gets homework from two schools. "Oh," said Billy. It made sense to him. There was always a lot of happiness when he was done. Billy celebrated the finish of his homework with joy, and he was filled with pride. He could then go on to watch a television show or a video. He didn't just watch it, he was enjoying a prize won by hard work.

I will be very good in my
new Spanish class.

1. I Will Be Very good in my
new Spanish Class.

2. I Will Be very good in My
New ~~X~~ Spanish Class,

3. I Will Be Very good in My
new spanish Class,

4. I Will ~~Spanish class~~ Be Very good
in My Spanish class,

5. I Will Be Very good in my Spanish
class,

6. I Will Be very good in My spanish class

7. I Will Be Very good inMy spanish class,

8. I Will Be Very good in My Spanish class,

PART II

Adjusting to a Non-Typical World

The book is about...

Monday

There are Dragons in a Valley,
They live peacefuly.
Their children are
friendly.

-
-
-

Tuesday

There was a King.
He ruled the noble
Planet was.
All he drinks
and eats is lemonade and
fuge

Wednesday

On the open there is a toad Who
is rich. He Wants to live
in a moving house. His fairote
hody is to drie moter
cans.

Chapter 7

In the debris of two minds

- A typical child is conscious of reality.

- Billy, most of the time, was not conscious of the world around him.

- My task: to begin to understand Billy's mind and to work to bring it closer to typical functioning.

Every school morning, at 9:15, I would call, "Class time!" Sometimes the call made Billy fuss; "Already! That's not fair!" But most of the time he would go obediently into our classroom and sit at his desk, waiting for me to teach him. He readily offered his physical presence. He did not, though, offer his mental presence quite so readily. During the 45 minutes of each class I would spend at least 20 gathering Billy's attention and attempting to focus him on a task.

At the beginning of the Aristotle School, my efforts to attract Billy's attention were mundane: calling his name many times, waving my hand in front of his eyes, clapping my hands. These methods, though, were not highly effective. They worked, but they took a lot of energy and I couldn't help feeling irritated by the fact that we lost so much time just organizing his mind. So I set out to educate myself about the mind. As it happened, I had to educate myself about not one mind, but two – and much more.

Indeed, we are all creatures of two minds, one conscious and one subconscious, one we are aware of and one not. The conscious mind is, in comparison with the subconscious one, pitifully limited. The conscious mind is the surface of the ocean. The subconscious mind is all that's hidden under that surface.

My faVorite show is Batman Because it has a gun.

Yet only thanks to the conscious mind's alertness can we connect with the world around us.

Most of us drift between one mind and the other with great ease. Daydreaming, we may become immersed in the depths of the subconscious mind. Then a car horn honks or the phone rings and the conscious mind yanks us back, startled. Leaping back and forth between the two minds comes naturally to most of us. But this leap does not come naturally to Billy. His conscious mind is often submerged, dragged down, in the depths of his subconscious.

The subconscious mind is powerful; it contains vast information and is magnificently artful in imagining. But imagination, while it serves us in many ways, does not dominate the lives of most of us. Imagination does dominate Billy's life. His is a fairytale-rich imagination, full of pictures, sounds and action.

Billy at six years was at home in his inner world, not in the surrounding world. As long as he had food and a few basic comforts, he would rather have spent his time in the vastness of his subconscious mind. He had no conception of time. The past was meaningless and so was the future, and prospects meant nothing to him. So he saw no incentive to work with the world of the present as a way to secure the future. But Billy's future prospects concerned us, his parents. In order to influence our boy's future, we had to pull him out of his inner world and connect him with the outer world. We had to fight for his attention, so that he could spend more time being conscious of the reality around him. We had to fight both for the attention of his conscious mind and for space in his subconscious mind. While his imagination wanted to keep the subconscious mind all for itself, we had to squeeze in to implant thoughts and images which reflected life in the world, in the United States, at the turn of the millennium.

Remember Mowgli, the jungle boy of Kipling's novel, raised by wolves? Billy was our Mowgli, reluctant to leave the jungle of his inner world, where he was content. We had no way to force him out. We could only lure him. The only way we could succeed was to find a way to make Billy begin to recognize the breadth and the beauty of the surrounding world, to seduce him with this beauty and make his conscious mind become more and more part of our world.

What we didn't know when we set this task was that in the process we in our turn would be seduced and lured by the jungle of Billy's imagination; that we would accept a time-sharing policy for what is real and what imagined; and that we would come to admire and participate in the world of Billy's imagination, seduced by its total freedom.

Chapter 8

Where are you, Billy?

- A typical child spends most of his time in the conscious mind, aware of and connected with the surrounding world.

- Billy spends most of his time in the depths of his subconscious mind, unaware of and unconnected with the surrounding world.

- My task: to understand the contents of his subconscious mind.

I started by asking Billy to describe what was in his mind. At first he was reluctant to talk about it. He certainly had a very poor vocabulary, but I didn't believe that to be the only reason for his non-communication. Small children manage to communicate happily even when all they can do is utter *a-g-u*-ing sounds.

I wondered if Billy's apprehension might be an acquired reaction, a result of his short life's experiences. Maybe, without any ill-intention, we had contributed to that apprehension. For one thing, we surely had not accepted his inner world. In fact, we'd been utterly rude in our attempts to pull him out of that world and to impose our reality on him. I came to understand all this when watching him, one-on-one, in the Aristotle School, and I decided to treat his inner world with respect even if it didn't make sense to me. I made an effort to be demonstrably gentle and engaging when I talked to Billy about his inner world.

"Billy, tell me, what story do you have in your mind now?"

"Oh, Mom. Nothing."

"I know there's a story. I bet it's a good one. I think it's about dolls."

"No, Mom, it's not about dolls, silly! It's about dragons."

"Dragons? How wonderful! I'd love to hear a story about dragons!"

"Really?"

"Yes, I would. I will sit here quietly and listen. What color is the dragon in your story, is he pink?"

"No, Mom, he is green. He is very kind and he has wings." As Billy started sharing his world with me, I realized just how "real" that world was for him. Billy's subconscious mind was (and still is) a mysterious world of castles, knights and dragons. There are deadly fights, there are evil spirits. Always, there's someone to be avenged, or someone to be saved. And in a middle of a most important rescue mission, we, the boy's well-meaning parents, have the audacity to insist that he should keep quiet or wash his hands!

I remembered myself when I was 15 years old and in love for the first time. A world opened inside me that was never there before, a world full of beauty and mystery. I longed for moments when I could just sit quietly and dream on, connecting with that world of pure magic. But reality always forced itself on me, most often in the form of my mother's urging voice: "Come on, wash the dishes" or "Clean up that mess right now!" Dirty dishes and messy rooms dragged me out of my magic world. I didn't throw temper tantrums. I only was sad. I wished my mother could understand, and could let me have some little time for aloneness. But I couldn't tell her about my new world. I was afraid she'd laugh at me.

Here I was doing the same thing to my boy, not honoring his dream world. And he was afraid to tell me about it, perhaps because he didn't want to be laughed at. It took me a while to gain Billy's trust, to get him to share with me what was in his hidden mind. When he realized he could actually talk with me about his knights and dragons, he began using every chance to tell his stories.

"Mom, do you think this dragon is real? Are you afraid of bad spirits? I need to tell you about this fight when the big, huge dragon goes to a far away land to fight mean spirits. There was a storm in his way. You know."

Now we have more stories than we ever wished for. We also have a much happier boy.

Chapter 9

Are you with me?

- A typical child drifts with ease between the conscious mind and the subconscious.

- Billy, once he is captured by his subconscious mind, becomes its prisoner.

- My task: to learn to bring Billy to his conscious mind quickly, but in a gentle and considerate way.

Most mornings, Billy's body came into the classroom, but his mind was still captivated in the jungle of his imagination. In order to teach him, I had to pull him out of that jungle and into conscious awareness. But what did I have to offer him as an alternative to his wonderland? A math problem? A worksheet with short and long vowels? Rules for capitalization? Could I ever compete with the excitement of his inner world? I needed to find a clever way to compete with Billy's subconscious mind.

I had already learned that Billy is glad when I pay homage to his inner world instead of ignoring it. So, as a working method, I imagined that Billy was watching a movie. If I were in a theater watching an extremely engaging movie and someone came in and told me to get out of there and do some math, I'd be upset, maybe extremely upset. I'd fight to stay on and finish watching. But I might agree to get out and do some math if I were assured that I could come back and finish the movie later. I'd just need to be certain that it would definitely happen, and when. I'd be even more agreeable to interrupting my viewing if I were told that, when I come back, I'll have pleasant company instead of watching the movie alone.

Applying this scheme in the classroom went like this. First, I'd ask Billy about the story in his mind. Next, I'd participate in developing it with him. If the story seemed to be near its end, we'd go on and finish it together. Then I'd ask him if he was ready for our class. Usually he answered, "Yes, I'm ready." If the story seemed to be at the beginning of its development, I'd bring it to a pause and ask Billy if it would be all right to come back to our class and to continue the story at our break time. Usually Billy would consent to this proposal, and we'd go on with our math or writing. When we finished the class, I always made sure to remind him that he could use his break time to finish his story.

This approach proved to be much more efficient than the one that I'd employed before of clapping my hands and calling "Billy, are you with me? Billy, are you with me?" only to admit to myself that he was not, in fact, with me. I realized that I couldn't reach out and bring Billy from his subconscious mind as a figure of authority, as a teacher. I had to become his equal, his accomplice in whatever adventure he was engaged in at the time. Together we worried about a noble knight. Together we witnessed a dragon spitting fire. Together, we made sure that the evil spirits were brought down. Then, also together, we moved on to learning some math.

Chapter 10

Minding the "D" words

- A typical child is expected to be receptive to the words "don't" and "stop", and, upon hearing them, to react in a very specific way.

- Billy, when confronted with these two most useful educational words, reacts to them in same way he reacts to the sound of a dishwasher or other background noise: the words are mere sounds. They have no meaning to him.

- My task: when I talk to Billy, to make myself heard and to learn how to influence his reactions.

While I was making a "List of Things to Work On" at the start of the Aristotle School, at the top of my list was: "How to talk to Billy." When parents speak to their children, they expect them to react in very specific ways, appropriate to the situation. If love is given to children, they are expected to enjoy it. If a scolding is being administered, the children are not expected to leap with joy. When the children are asked to "stop" or are told "don't," they are expected to discontinue their actions.

I knew how to talk to children, but I knew how to talk to a typical child, not to Billy. My typical way of talking worked well with Francesca. As a rule, I never needed more than three prompts, at most, to make her pay attention to me:

- "Francesca, I need to talk to you."

- "Stop reading. Don't look at the book. Look at me."

- "Now listen."

The first prompt gets the girl into a state of mild alertness combined with mild resistance; the second gets her to succumb to the inevitable; and the third makes her face me and acknowledge my existence. There's still the matter of whether she'll hear and/or comprehend what I have to say, but that's another question.

This approach had quite a different effect upon Billy. With Billy, a three-step alert call left him as unaffected as it would leave a seal sleeping on the ocean beach. If Billy was reading a book and I tried one-two-three on him, he remained as engrossed in his reading as if I didn't exist. My voice was just a part of the background, carrying no more meaning than the dish-washer's noise.

It was of course obvious to me that Billy's atypical reactions were, at least in part, a consequence of his autism. That understanding was well settled; but it had settled only in the left side of my brain, the one that contained my abilities, however mediocre, to be logical and reasonable. The right side of my brain comported itself as if it knew nothing of Billy's condition. With that side of my brain I only saw a child who did not pay attention to me and did not give a damn about what I said.

We learn early in our lives to be upset when someone pays no attention to us. It's so painful to be ignored. It's so comfortable to act in the same way as my mother did before me, and my grandmother before her. Yet I had to disrupt this continuity of conduct. Somehow, if I wanted to manage an atypical child, I had to become an atypical parent. This meant that I had to ignore his "lack of respect for me" as well as my emotional pain at being treated like the dishwasher.

Appealing to the left side of my brain for authority, I began coaxing my right brain into the belief that the only pains that made sense were those which have a prospect of a cure. Since my wounded feelings had proved to be of no value in managing Billy, they had to go. I had to deconstruct my whole attitude about the dynamics of parent–child communications.

It made sense to be upset at Francesca when she didn't pay attention to me, because I could get her to feel guilty about it, to accept it as wrongdoing and attempt to do better in the future. It didn't make sense to be upset at Billy. The day came when I felt quite stupid doing that, because there was no way I could cause in him a feeling of guilt about not listening to me. I couldn't make him accept it as wrongdoing and get him to commit to a path of improvement. He had no clue what on earth I wanted from him. He was just sitting quietly and reading.

In my book *The Dragons of Autism* there is a chapter called "Don't Say Don't," where I wrote about the lack of information that is supplied to the brain by the word "don't." When we hear someone saying "Don't be a pig!" the word "pig" puts much more information into our brain than the word "don't." That's why a natural reaction to "Don't be a pig!" is "Yes! I am a pig! And I'll keep being a pig!" – assuming that "Don't be a pig" is said to an unintimidated opponent.

Most children are, to their parents, intimidated opponents. They are very early on trained that "Don't!" means the same thing as a red light at a busy intersection. If they manage to be good and enforce the "Don't!" on themselves, their parents will be pleased. Life will be OK. If they ignore the "Don't!" there is a high possibility of a clash of wills, during the course of which the children may have to endure damage of one kind or another. The children learn to avoid such clashes by obeying the "Don'ts". When they hear, "Don't push!" "Don't scream!" "Don't you dare!" they react accordingly, trying to find a way to deal with their own impulses while also trying to avoid making a parent cross.

The words "Billy" and "intimidation" make an oxymoron. With Billy we had to acknowledge the impotence of our attempts to transform him into an intimidated opponent. Billy could not be intimidated. His brain refused to make the connections necessary to make "Don't!" work. We couldn't make him connect his behavior to our reactions. When we told him "Don't," he ignored it. Not because: one – he heard us; two – he understood what was being asked of him; three – he chose to disobey. He ignored the "Don't!" because to him it had no meaning whatsoever. His brain couldn't manage to transform the command "Don't scream!" into a self-induced decision to be silent.

A typical child manages to figure out that when parents say "Don't scream!" they are in fact saying, "Be quiet!" rather then "Go jump from the roof!" Billy in this situation couldn't figure out by himself what was expected of him. His brain wasn't capable of making a quick analysis of a situation to produce a desirable (to the parent) interpretation of "Don't!" We needed to learn to tell Billy not what *not* to do, but instead what we wanted him to do. "Don't spill!" had to be transformed into "Keep your eyes on your cup." "Don't scratch!" into "Clap your hands!" and "Don't stand in front of the TV!" into "Sit down!"

In the classroom, this meant that I needed to find substitutes for "Don't talk without permission!" "Don't look out the window!" "Don't chew on your pencil!" "Don't wrinkle the page!" "Don't scratch the desk!" and all the rest. In time, as Billy's vocabulary increased, I managed to teach him that the world of people is filled by many patterns of action and by reactions to them. He became susceptible, somewhat, to "don'ts." Yet still, the chance of having him follow our words with desirable conduct is much better if we use a positive suggestion and tell him what we want him to do.

You see, Billy knows only "doing." If you think of it, what is not doing? It's an abstract notion, because no matter what, we keep doing something. We certainly keep being alive, breathing, feeling. If a mind has a detailed awareness, a detailed map, of the surrounding reality, then at a "Don't!" command the mind may find it easy enough to figure out where it should go on the map. But what if the mind is fully immersed in one activity at a time? What if it has no map of the surrounding reality? If, at a given time, there's nothing else but "running with a cup in hand" and then suddenly there's "Don't spill!", how does one go about it, about that not spilling?

It's not easy to avoid "don'ts." When looking for alternatives, I try to make sure that, first of all, I use words which are in Billy's vocabulary. Then I need to imagine the workings of Billy's brain to find a command that will have a practical meaning and will get him to react in a particular way. Knowing that, in fact, Billy does not like spilling drinks on the floor, I tell him, "Keep your eyes on the cup!" Because if he keeps his eyes on the cup he will automatically try to keep from spilling. Also, because spilling occurs when he moves fast, my command would be even better if I said "Go slow, eyes on the cup. Slow, small steps, eyes on the cup, please."

Thus commenced my quest to become an atypical parent. The quest is still on, a daily test of my dedication. There are occasional thrills, when I manage to scale yet another atypical height. When I started training myself to rid my speech of that meager combination of one tiny word and a piece of another – "Don't"– I thought I would

I'm good at-
pictures of dragons
and dinos I'm also
good at reading
adventure books.

be clean in no time. But high hopes came too quickly. Two years later, I still struggle with "Don't." In our family, we now call it the "D" word. We catch each other using it more frequently than we expected, but we do laugh when one of us says, "Don't say the 'D' word!"

Soon after I started my rebellion against the "D" word, I became aware how frequently this word appears in the parent–child vocabulary. Now, in playgrounds or school grounds or in television programs, I can't help but notice the shower of "Don'ts" that pours over our children. It's pathetic. Yet I still do it myself. The main reason we use "Don't" so much is that it's easy. We see the child doing something, and we react just by naming that very "doing" and adding a "Don't." The brain of the parent can thus react without having to think.

The reason it's so hard to use alternatives is that the alternatives require the brain to do work under stressful circumstances. Usually, when we say "Don't!" we want an immediate reaction. We are not inclined to take time to search for an eloquent approach to an urgent situation. When the kid is digging in the dirt, it's quicker to say "Don't" than to suggest an alternative.

In learning to use positive suggestions, it helps that the daily routine of child-raising ordinarily involves relatively few situations, and most of them predictable. The times when the urge to say "Don't" arises are usually the same ones over and over; they are about not being mean, not messing up, about putting things away and keeping out of danger. So once a vocabulary of positive suggestions is built, it's only a matter of time before the right words come easily at the right time.

There is one more word which I interpret as a "negative suggestion." It's the word "Stop." Telling Billy to stop was like telling a tornado to stop. The word failed to trigger the reactions in Billy's brain that we expected it to trigger, that is:

- to understand that he was to interrupt a certain activity

- to agree to interrupt that activity

- to cause his bodily parts to interrupt the activity.

I speculated, based on my observations of Billy, that his brain was so engrossed in an activity that it had no room for processing steps one, two and three. Without that process he could not possibly arrive at the point at which I wanted him to arrive – that is, actually stopping what he was doing. He simply couldn't make himself stop doing something "now". He couldn't stop hitting, or pushing, or scratching.

As I said, it's like telling a tornado to stop, or telling the driver of a moving car. The car will not stop immediately. The driver has to move his foot, press the brakes, and then some more time elapses before the car finally stops. But what if there's a dangerous obstacle in front of the car? Then the situation changes. The reaction of the driver is much quicker, and his alertness is vastly elevated. Pressing the brakes plus stopping may not be the optimal reaction. Maybe it's better to turn the car in a different direction, if there is one.

I found that I was more likely to cause Billy to stop one activity if I gave him a quick suggestion to do something else. Just as with the "Don'ts," the "Stops" had to go, to make space for positive suggestions.

I'm learning that instead of saying "Stop writing on the wall!" I can say "Take this paper and draw a dragon for me." Instead of saying "Stop bothering me!" I can say "I need your help to set up the table." Instead of saying "Stop hiding under the bed!" I can say "Please hide in the closet." Instead of saying "Stop splashing!" I can say "Show me how you sail the red boat in the water."

You can see that the "Stop!" sentences come with an exclamation point, reflecting the general mood with which such sentences are pronounced. The alternatives, interestingly, have a more subdued emotional charge. The "Stops!" are about imposing and dominating. The alternatives are more about understanding and cooperating.

Chapter 11

Eye language

- A typical child likes to stare at people. Much of a child's social learning comes from mere looking.

- Billy avoids people's eyes.

- My task: to teach Billy to enjoy looking at people.

How often, when describing a loved one, people start in the same place – they start by talking about eyes! "Her eyes, mysterious and distant!" "His eyes, reflecting light and magic!"

Our parents, raising us, make sure that we learn to communicate not just through speech but through body language too. We are taught not only to be aware of what we say, but also when not to pick our nose; but we are rarely made aware of eye language. Yet this is one of our most important means of communication. The eyes can be angry or strict, accusing or praising, mocking or compassionate, questioning or approving, gentle or loving, exalted or ecstatic, and much, much more than that.

In large part this is probably because every typical person understands basic eye language intuitively, without any formal training. We don't take eye language classes. We learn it without thinking; it just comes to us, effortlessly. We learn it by imitating those around us, in the same way that our basic verbal language comes to us as children.

Children can learn a verbal language perfectly well without a single lesson in grammar or syntax. But to teach a language, one must be able to sort it out, to be able to separate verbs from nouns and correct pronunciations from incorrect. (You should hear me sometimes trying to teach Billy English, with my Russian accent – like the difference between "shorts" and "shirts." "Oh, Mom, we don't say it *that* way!")

Eye language, too, is typically passed from generation to generation without conscious guidance. But the traditional ways of learning eye language did not work for Billy. He did not imitate his mother and father. Actually, he did not look at people at all, so for him there was nothing to imitate.

I had to teach myself how to teach eye language. I started by trying to imagine what Billy might possibly be gaining by avoiding people's eyes. Only one guess made sense to me: he avoids eyes in order to protect his inner world. I thought about myself and tried to remember under what circumstances I avoided people's eyes. Number one, of course, is when I don't want to admit the truth. Also, when I want to hide my thoughts, when I don't want them to become available to another party, when I don't want someone to witness my inner world, whatever it may hide.

Number two, I hide my eyes when I want to be left alone. Putting my eyes down means unwillingness to participate in a conversation. After that come the times when we are caught up in our own thoughts, when we are remembering things, imagining things, creating things. The bottom line is that when we look into someone's eyes we automatically engage that person, whether he wants it or not, in eye-to-eye communication. We automatically start speaking, but we speak in eye language. Like any communication, eye language requires attention and energy. If we want to concentrate on an inner process, we keep our eyes from engaging in eye language. And so does Billy.

My first step in teaching Billy eye language was aimed at making him accept at least one bit of it. I thought of that first bit as jumping on an unruly horse. Once on it, I hoped, we would move with the wind! The first bit of eye language that Billy accepted came through a very simple exercise. I called it the OM exercise. It goes as follows.

We sit on stools, facing each other. Billy's stool is higher than mine so that our eyes are at approximately the same level. Then we move our heads toward each other, keeping our eyes locked on one another's eyes, until our foreheads almost touch. While we move toward each other we say, "O-O-O-O-M."

(There is no magic in the sound itself. I learned to use it in yoga meditation, and I find it soothing and like how it vibrates in the chest.)

When our foreheads are almost touching, we move back into an upright position on our stools. Then we repeat the movement. Since Billy functions much better in an environment in which limits are set very clearly, we agree in advance on the number of times we will do OM. We usually start with ten and raise fingers to keep track of our progress. Sometimes we have so much fun that we go for another ten, or even for another two tens.

How did I sell OM to Billy? I asked him if he wanted to do a very funny exercise with me.

"What is it?" he asked.

"It's an exercise in which I lose one eye. How many eyes do I have?"

"Mom, don't be silly, you have two eyes."

"That's correct. But I can show how I have only one eye."

"How?" asked Billy, obviously curious.

"Well…Let's sit on these stools. We'll move our heads toward each other and say O-O-O-O-M. But you have to hold your eyes on mine all the time while you move your head. Can you do that?"

"I think so," said Billy.

It's true that when you get your heads very close together, but still keep your eyes locked, you cease to see both eyes. You see only a distorted version of two eyes, superimposed on each other in a surreal one eye–two irises image. It's fascinating and quite entertaining.

We did OM every day in our class for about three months. By the end of those three months, I saw a dramatic improvement in Billy's eye contact. I was on the horse!

Meanwhile I started to train myself in the grammar and syntax of eye language. I needed to become good at making different kinds of expressions with my eyes, so that I could demonstrate those differences to Billy in a way that made them apparent to him. I ought to say that you may find it hard to teach eye language if you're worried about looking ridiculous.

In my youth, I had my share of times when I felt stupid after acting ridiculous, and so for years I worked hard to cultivate a dignified air. Now to teach eye language to Billy I had to learn to drop that act and look ridiculous again. But frankly, there is a difference between acting ridiculous because you don't know any better and acting ridiculous because you intend to. You want the second option, that's for sure.

"Billy, Mom is going to give you a goodnight kiss. OK?"

"OK."

"I'm thinking, should I give you a fierce eyes kiss, like this [fierce eyes follow], or should I give you a sweety-pie eyes kiss [sweety-pie eyes follow]."

"Sweety-pie eyes kiss."

I made sure that the fierce eyes looked really fierce, even though this was impossible to do without distorting the whole face into an unappealing conglomerate of facial parts. After that treat, the sweety-pie eyes looked like a real refuge. No wonder Billy went for them.

"Billy, you didn't do your homework. I think we should look into each other's eyes."

"No, Mom. I don't think so."

"Why not? Because you know my eyes are angry?"

"Mom, you need to be kind."

"OK, I will be kind. And you will do your homework."

"OK."

"Good. Now I have kind eyes. See?" We hug, and Billy looks into my kind eyes.

Our eye language training is still in process. Billy's command of it is pretty good with people whom he knows well. A new person is still too much of an enigma for him, too complex to decipher. So he saves his energy by not looking.

In the Russian language there is a saying "Do you wish to kick someone out of your heart? Move him out of your eyesight!" Billy used to operate this saying in reverse. By not letting us into his eyesight, he was not letting us into his heart. Now, after our eye language training, Billy's heart is wonderfully open. We can make all kinds of eyes, but the ones he likes best are the loving ones.

Chapter 12

Body language

- A typical child automatically learns to use the body language of the culture in which he or she is brought up.

- Billy uses a body language that is clearly alien to our culture. We find it largely inappropriate and so do other people.

- My task: to help him align his body language with what is considered socially acceptable.

It's likely that you've heard about "the mind–body connection." An army of New Age adepts educate us about it. They tell us that a person may become depressed (mind) as a result of a hemorrhoid (body); that another person may become healthy (body) as a result of ardent prayer (mind).

Understanding the mind–body connection is crucial in the practice of hypnotherapy. The method most widely used to put a person into a hypnotic trance is "progressive relaxation." At first the therapist ensures that all of the client's muscles are very relaxed. Amazingly enough, the mind follows the muscles, just like a cat's tail follows its body. The mind relaxes, its waves slowing down to a place where the person is not even capable of thinking.

The reverse is true as well: an agitated mind translates itself into agitated muscles. Sometimes this muscle agitation is not obvious. In some people who are very much in control of themselves, the body does not betray their inner intensity. For other people, agitation of mind may easily translate into agitated body language. The stereotypical television Italian is prone to express his thoughts through body language; the Clint Eastwood cowboy won't. Different strokes for different folks, right?

Everything wasn't quite right with Billy's body language. There was so much of it and it took such odd forms that we couldn't think of any culture on this earth where it would seem appropriate. Before Billy had eye language and verbal language at his command, he had only his body as a means of interacting with other people. Billy did many things which other children do as a part of exploring the world. But where other children measured their explorations against the reactions of adults, Billy, whose person-to-person skills were impaired, had to do explore the world by trial and error. He was a scientist alone on an island and having to discover fire all over again. Out of touch with humanity, Billy could rely only on his bodily experiences to explore the world. It was no wonder that this engaged his body in a succession of continuous and elaborate movements.

He learned that if he opened the white door in the kitchen, there was ice cream behind it. He learned that if his mother was around, she made him put the ice cream box back behind the white door. He learned that if his mother was not around, he was not made to put the ice cream box behind the white door. Naturally, he concluded that he should go for the ice cream when his mother was not around.

Billy loved to do things that had an immediate physical result, omitting all other means of communication. These included pushing people, dropping things on the floor, playing with doors, scratching things, spitting on windows and smearing it around, splashing, banging, hitting, squeezing, waving, circling, stomping. He used his body to be in touch with the world.

We tried to stop him from doing that, thinking that we were trying to stop him from misbehaving. In fact, we were limiting his interactions with the world, such as they were. In fact, we were imposing behavioral prohibitions on Billy while offering nothing in return. I started to gain a glimpse of Billy's mind–body connection while working with him closely in our Aristotle School. There, little by little, I came to perceive Billy's erratic body movements as a body language all of his own. I also came to regret every "Billy! Don't do that!" which he'd had to endure.

In the long run, since Billy's body language was all he had to rely on, his use of it became quite skillful. What would you do if you wanted to play dragons? Ask nicely for someone to play with you, right? Billy, though, didn't know how to ask. Instead, he made his body into the picture of a dragon. He brought his jaw down and showed all his teeth, he bent his back, he made his fingers like claws and he walked the most magnificent dragon walk one could ever put together! Anybody out there to appreciate it?

The reaction to this masterful performance was usually not the one he was hoping for. Frightened children ran to their mommas. The displeased mommas asked me to control my boy. Then I'd try to put enough disciplinary impact in my voice to assure the mommas that I, in my turn, was not about to tolerate Billy's act.

"Billy, put your hands down! Do you hear what I said? Put your hands down right now!" But by telling him to put his hands down I was depriving him of his only means of communication. And it was not fair to do so without first supplying him with another means of communication.

As we progressed in learning eye language and verbal language, Billy began to rely less and less on his body language to communicate. But still his body was always in motion, as if incapable of separating itself from his thoughts.

Imagine that your body has to move one way or another every time a thought crosses your mind. Perhaps you'll remain quiet when you're engrossed in reading, generating no thoughts of your own, or when you're asleep, but that's about it. Unless you're a yogi, hidden in a cave and deep in a trance, your mind is generating thoughts nearly all the time. With your thoughts shuffling like a deck of cards in the hands of good player, your body will be jerked here and there as if by a series of electric shocks. And that's an exact picture of Billy. His body moved more or less all the time except when he was reading or asleep. His body moved continuously in our classroom. His feet did a little dance on the floor, his hands searched for something to hold, his fingers looked for something to roll. For a self-proclaimed teacher, that was distressing, to put it mildly.

So I began a hunt. My quarry was not Billy's body language: my quarry was his awareness of his body language. That awareness was lost, or perhaps it was never there. My task was to find it, capture it, train it and put it to good use.

The first thing that I did was to make a weight vest for Billy. I was told I could buy one, but I opted for making one myself. The weight vests that I saw in Theresa's class were made out of stiff twill fabric, usually of a dark solid color. I made one of soft cotton, with colorful lizards pictured on it. It looked cool. Billy thought it made him look like a knight. In fact, watching how he enjoyed wearing it, and becoming aware how much the vest calmed his body, I thought I might enjoy one myself.

The vest, though, didn't take care of his feet so I started using on Billy the ankle weights which I had bought for myself to enhance the impact of my walking exercises. Billy loved the ankle weights as well, and they did help to calm and control his dancing feet.

So we proceeded to put on all those weights before every class. At first I was bothered by the association that kept popping up in my mind – chains hanging on prisoners as they were led to Siberian exile. But then I've found a nicer way to describe our weight-hanging procedure: I was "grounding" Billy. It gave me a spiritual justification for the weight hanging and a way of talking about it with Billy. Indeed, after "grounding" Billy was noticeably more "grounded." He was more in touch with earthly things and a bit less in touch with his wild inner world.

Again, it wasn't that his inner world didn't matter to me, but if I left his mind prey to his inner world, he would never fit easily into the earthly world. In fact Billy didn't want to alienate himself from our world. He did have earthly dreams, such as his dream of having a restaurant when he grows up. Fascinated by the French fries from Denny's restaurant, Billy dreamed of having his own food parlor – "Billy's." And Billy shared with me that he thought he'd have three children – one good girl, whose projected name was invariably Rose, and twin boys. The boys were projected to be naughty, and their names changed regularly from Tom and Tommy to Hike and Bike.

I was determined to do anything I could to increase the chance that Billy's earthly dreams might come true; even if his twin boys were projected to be naughty; even if Billy thought that it was me who would teach them to be good. "Mom," he'd say, "You're good at discipline." In his scheme of how the world turns, boys, unlike girls, couldn't just be born good. Boys had to be taught to be good. Would I ever go back to quilting?

So we had our first small success in making Billy aware of his body. He become aware that the weights gave him comfort and made his body move less. There were days when I'd ask Billy to sit at his desk and, with a lesson plan on my mind, I'd forget about the weights. But he always remembered about them as soon as his bottom touched the chair, as if indeed he felt that there wasn't enough "grounding" to "ground" him to the chair. "Whoops! My weights! Mom, you forgot!" he'd say and rush to put on his "knightly" attire.

Although the weights were useful, they were not a very convenient tool. We were glad to use them in the privacy of the Aristotle School, but we did not feel comfortable having the weights on Billy in public places – not at Denny's, certainly. I needed other means to build Billy's awareness of his body. Over several months I came up with a number of exercises that I hoped would make Billy aware of his movements. Some of them didn't do much for us, but a few were a quick hit. Billy liked to do them, I saw an immediate benefit from them, and the benefit increased as we kept doing those exercises.

Amazingly enough, all the useful body-awareness exercises were very simple. Billy benefited from them as he accumulated repeated experience over a long period of time. These body-awareness exercises (and many other exercises Billy has done as well) have what I call a "cast effect." I've seen children whose legs were put in a cast to correct some imperfection, but the cast didn't work overnight. In fact, it didn't work "overweek" or "overmonth" either. It takes a long, long time to make a bone grow in a new way, to make all the cells assume a new pattern.

I didn't have to change the way Billy's bones were growing but I had to change the way his mind worked. Being aware that minds can be as stiff as bones (I had my own mind, at some times in my life, as a good example), I figured that changing the works of Billy's mind might take a long, long time, and then only if we had a cast on it. We couldn't buy a cast for Billy's mind. The only possible cast was my will to persist in making Billy do the same exercises over and over and over, day by day, week by week, month by month, until his brain cells would assume a new pattern of behavior.

My intention was to make Billy aware of his bodily parts and the way they move, and also aware of the speed and of a possible emotional charge in his movements. Ultimately, we did five major groups of exercises:

1. Clapping.
2. Gentle movements.
3. Posture training.
4. Facial training.
5. Gesture language.

Clapping

We started by doing the simplest clapping, in which each partner claps his or her own hands (on the count of one), and then the partners clap hands with one another (on the count of two).

When we started this exercise, Billy, although excited and eager to do it, made continuous mistakes. He forgot to clap his hands, or he clapped them twice, or he missed my hands. After about four weeks, though, we became very good at it, clapping fast and with no mistakes for a good stretch of time, one to two minutes and then four to five minutes.

Meanwhile, we developed more elaborate versions of clapping. In a matter of about three months we had an arsenal of clapping versions. The most complicated ones had 15 or more movements. Here is a 15-movement version:

1. Partners clap their own hands.

2. Clap only one of the partner's hands, on diagonal.

3. Partners clap their own hands.

4. Clap the other hand of the partner, on diagonal.

5. Partners clap their own hands.

6. Partners clap each other's hands, parallel.

7. Partners clap their own hands.

8. Partners clap their own shoulders, criss-cross.

9. Partners clap their own hands.

10. Partners clap each other's hands, parallel.

11. Partners clap their own hands.

12. Partners clap one of their own knees with the opposite hand.

13. Partners clap their own hands.

14. Partners clap their other knee with the opposite hand.

15. Partners clap their own hands.

Clapping exercises became a time of good fun for both of us. I loved seeing the progress Billy made. Over time, he became faster and better coordinated. He also wanted to design his own versions of clapping. I let him do that up to the point where, invariably, he got entangled in the dilemma of not having enough body parts available to satisfy his creativity.

Gentle movements

While I was working on Billy's body language, I'd often use the word "gentle." "Billy, be gentle to the children!" "Billy, move gently!" and so on.

If my attempts to incorporate gentleness into Billy's manners brought progress, it was invisible. Then one day I asked him, "Billy, what does the word 'gentle' mean?" "I don't know," was the answer. At moments like this I just try to breathe deeply. I have to breathe through the feeling of being an idiot who is teaching algebra without taking the trouble to inquire whether the student has ever learned arithmetic.

So I've learned that before I try to teach Billy anything I need to make sure that he has an idea of the meaning of the words I'll be using. Now, as Billy's vocabulary has increased after two years of Aristotle School, I can explain to him the meaning of one word by using other words, words that he already knows. Even now Billy learns much faster from a dramatized demonstration than from a verbal explanation.

We worked on the meaning of the word "gentle" for quite some time. He got the concept right away, but we needed to reinforce it over and over before his brain reacted immediately. I still work with Billy, from time to time, to reinforce the word "gentle". Our procedure is simple:

1. We sit next to each other. I pull up the sleeve of Billy's shirt above his elbow. Then I turn his arm so that his palm faces up, exposing the very tender inner part of the arm.

2. Next I move my finger sharply from his wrist to the middle of his arm. "Is that a gentle move?" I ask. "No," Billy answers, as expected.

3. Then I move a finger again from the wrist to the middle of his arm, but this time very slowly and tenderly. "Does that feel good and gentle, Billy?" "Yes," comes the answer.

4. "Now you take a finger on your other hand and put it on your wrist. And I will put my finger there too. We will keep our eyes locked on our fingers. We will move our fingers together from your wrist to the middle of your arm. We start moving when I say 'one.' We finish only when I say 'fifteen' and not before."

5. "See, Billy, that's what it means to move gently."

Needless to say, during our first attempts at this exercise Billy's finger "got out of hand" and reached the middle of his arm quickly, by the count of five or six.

"O-o-oops," I'd say, "Start again!" Little by little, Billy's finger learned to slow down as he let himself be mesmerized by the tender sensation on his arm while I, like an exotic soft-voiced parrot, repeated; "This is what it means to be gentle, Billy. That's to be gentle."

Posture training

This exercise trains a response to the words "Student posture, please." I taught Billy that student posture consists of four parts:

1. *Feet flat.* That means that his feet are flat on the floor next to each other, rather than on top of each other or spread in a little dangling dance.

2. *Hands flat.* That means that both hands are on the table, one resting on top of the other, palms down.

3. *Back straight.* That means his back is straight.

4. *Chin up.* As Billy raises his chin, he also makes eye contact with his teacher.

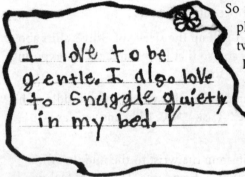

I love to be gentle. I also love to snuggle quietly in my bed.

So now when I say "Student posture, please. What's number one? Number two? Number three? Number four?" Billy gives all the answers correctly and arranges his body accordingly. It took about three or four months to master this process, but it has surely paid off.

Can he hold the student posture for long? No. But by now he is so used to reacting to the reminder "Student posture, please" that by hearing it he almost automatically rearranges his body to fit the requirements. In this way we have trained Billy's brain to respond almost immediately to a command that triggers a certain organization of his body. During the course of a class I may resort to this reminder quite a few times, yet because he's reached an almost automatic response it does not disrupt the thread of the class.

This training brought me a lot of joy because it allowed us to move beyond doing something "right" or "wrong," beyond judgments and accusations. It allowed for respectable reminders from my side and knowing reactions from Billy. Where before we had "Don't lean on the desk!" "Don't pick your nose!" "Don't slide off the chair!", now we have one simple request for "Student posture, please." When his body assumes the student posture, his mind automatically assumes a student posture as well.

Facial training

A poster sold by many educational supply stores depicts a dozen or so cute kiddy faces, each of them illustrating a different emotion and identifying each emotion with a word. We have that poster in the house. I bought it when Billy was about four, hoping that it would raise his awareness of facial expressions in general and his own facial expressions.

The poster went up in Billy's room. But his identification of facial expressions did not improve. I thought that maybe this was because we didn't spend much time in his room and therefore didn't go over the poster as often as we should have. So I moved the poster to the bathroom downstairs. I figured that if every time Billy goes to the bathroom he has to focus his attention on the poster, we'd be rolling.

We didn't roll. When Billy went to the bathroom, he went to the bathroom. It may well be that he is in the process of approaching maturity, so I may soon witness the development of one of the traits that make a man a man – the ability to read while attending to his bodily needs.[1] At nine he was still in too much of a hurry to get out of the bathroom and do things which aren't quite doable in a bathroom – build castles, or point swords at imagined foes.

Now, after spending many a moment pondering about Billy's doings and not doings, I'm amused at my early hopes for the poster. He wasn't even potty trained when I bought it. If I could not pull his awareness out of his subconscious maelstrom even for the purpose of reading the movements of his own bowels, he certainly was not ready for reading a poster, and especially not for such obscure reading as facial expressions.

I thought that faces made obscure reading for Billy when I started training him, but as I observed him, and I tried to look at people's faces with his eyes, I began to think that he might have very different reasons for avoiding faces. Since then, I've learned that reading facial expressions can be not just difficult but downright scary.

And I dreamed of my childhood. I saw myself, a little girl, standing in front of my mother who was busy scolding me and holding herself close in the formality of her fancy silk Chinese robe. What was she scolding me for? I couldn't remember, and I couldn't remember my mother's face. But I could remember my awareness that her face was scary. So my eyes looked toward her, but they did not see her. They looked beyond her. My eyes were capturing the silhouette of my nanny, who was standing silent by the door. I let my eyes

---

1   At nine and a half, he finally became an ardent bathroom reader.

become aware of my nanny's face. My nanny's face was not scary. In fact, it was quite funny as, behind my mother's back, she made silent clown faces to cheer me up. Something in me was laughing happily at her antics. Yet my body, displaying a self-learned wisdom, did nothing to betray my nanny's presence. My nanny was wise and fearless.

It was in the USSR of 1961, at the peak of communist power and glory, but the ghost of communism was not cruising Europe by then. It had settled comfortably in the USSR, inhabiting men with serious faces. Every day our mailwoman brought the newspapers for my communist father. He read them line by line, and his face looked just like the faces of the men in the pictures in the papers. Those were faces in which one could read readiness to forsake everything for the good of the party: family, love, children, everything.

My nanny brought the newspapers from the mailbox into the house, handling them with quiet care. Then when my father had finished ingesting yet another portion of censored texts, the papers were passed back to my nanny. She cut them into pieces of a size convenient to serve as toilet paper – a temporary solution to one of life's little needs while we waited for the country's industry to achieve communist glory in toilet paper.

My nanny loved this chore. She'd take me out to our old walnut tree and we'd settle under its protection. Holding a sharp knife, her fingers danced confidently while she sliced the paper. "Here goes Khrushchev!" she'd exclaim cheerfully, amused at the way that mighty man's picture was to be used. But I was not amused by the pictures of Khrushchev and other men who looked like my father. They all scared me so. If I had to look at one of them, I tried to look beyond them. In the outhouse I made sure to use only the pieces of paper that had no pictures.

My journey into adulthood passed through a forest of people with serious faces. As I grew up, I couldn't shake off the urge to hide from those faces. I hid, with a book or without one, whenever I could – at first among the branches of our walnut tree, then in my school homework, which I voluntarily doubled so I could spend more time at it. After that, I forgot how to hide and I went through some scary years until I learned how to hide within myself. That was the safest place of all, but it took so, so long to get there. Billy was born with a ready knowledge of how to hide within himself. He hid from all our adult faces filled with worries and concerns.

Once I made an attempt to look at contemporary American faces through the eyes of that little girl who couldn't use pictures of serious men in the outhouse because they scared her. What I saw scared me, just like in the old times. Lots of tired, serious faces. Lots of fake smiles. Lots of fear. Pain. Indifference. Disillusion. And that's just looking at faces in America.

Then I thought of looking at my own face with the eyes of that little girl, I *really* scared myself. God Almighty! While I was attempting to teach facial awareness to an autistic boy, I had no clue how to be aware of my very own face. So I began teaching myself to be aware of my face. At first I sat in front of the mirror, acquainting myself with my repertoire of facial expressions. Three-fourths of that repertoire had to go. I didn't like it, and I couldn't expect my children to like it. "Mirror, mirror, on the wall..." I used the mirror to find some new, pleasant alignments for the muscles of my face. Then I tried to master them so that they became a part my repertoire of facial expressions.

While I'm not a body builder, I am dedicated to exercising, but nothing of what I've put myself through before, from standing on my head to swimming in an ice hole, came close to that facial training. It took a long time to learn to be aware of my face and what it portrays. I'm still in the process of learning.

At some point I started teaching faces to Billy. I showed him funny faces, surprised faces, silly faces, loving faces, tricky faces. He loved all of them. Then I showed him an angry face. He jumped from his little stool in front of me, grabbed my cheeks with his little hands and started pushing them, as if kneading dough, saying, "Mom, please, Mom. No angry face, Mom, please!"

If my little boy had been a baker and could knead the dough of all the human faces on the earth, he'd work and work until he'd made sure that all the faces were kneaded into soft peaceful buns, looking like festive Czech strudels. He'd make all the faces look so good, one would want to eat them up!

These days when Billy looks beyond someone's face, I think of myself as a little girl, looking beyond my mother's face and seeing what she had no way of seeing. I could see the magic of my nanny's face, but that magic was open only to me. My mother stood with her back toward it. Even if she had turned around, the magic would not have been there. She would have had to become just like me to see it.

What is Billy seeing when he looks into his own beyond? Whatever is there, it is open only to him. I remain oblivious to it, maybe because it's not meant for me, or maybe because without even knowing it I have turned my back on it. One good day I might be able to let myself become just like Billy, so that when he looks beyond our world I can look with him and see the magic, and the magic will not vanish.

Gesture language

As with words, Billy did not follow the easy path of learning gestures by mim-
icking adults. Yet by the time he was four, he had mastered enough of the
language of gestures to get by. He spoke almost no words then. He used
gestures to communicate. Billy used, with great certainty, the gestures that are
associated with the word "no". His body knew how to say "yes", "I want this",
"open", and "close". So why train him? Number one, because he was not aware
of his gestures. They came wildly like bowel movements happen to babies.
Number two, because he displayed many gestures which most people would
interpret as unfriendly or threatening. Number three, because he did not
understand or use gestures that convey politeness and respect. Our training
comprised three parts:

1.   In the beginning there must be a word.

2.   One word is not enough.

3.   The theatre.

In the beginning there must be a word

So we started our gesture training "in the beginning" introducing the word
"gesture." According to the Random House dictionary, a gesture is "a
movement of the body, head, arms, hands or face that is expressive of an idea,
opinion, emotion, etc." We read the definition together and then we talked
about it, using simpler words and gesture-related concepts.

Gesture is a difficult word, yet not inconceivably difficult. It is no more
difficult then "subtraction" or "multiplication." It took Billy less than a week
to learn it. For several days I asked him to write the definition of the word on
paper, several times each day. We repeated the word over and over until it
finally sank into his brain.

One word is not enough

After learning that there are gestures, we had to learn that there are many
kinds of gestures. We undertook one of our first tasks of comprehensive classification. We learned that gestures could be:

- polite

- respectful

- kind

- playful

- invitational

- threatening

- angry.

I understand that my system of classification could be improved, but it served me sufficiently while I was teaching Billy.

The theatre

At last we reached the most engaging part: acting out the gestures. In our school I introduced a body-language class. It was fully dedicated to understanding body movements and what they communicated. I pretended to be a fine lady, and Billy was a knight who treats a lady with utmost respect. I pretended to be a cowboy who uses his hat to make a point. We practiced different ways of folding our bodies into a no or into a yes.

Billy got so excited by the whole thing that he started making some very complicated movements with his arms, asking me to guess what the gesture meant. I couldn't figure out the trick and told him that I gave up, asking him to tell me the answer. What I got for an answer was Billy's sweet and utterly bewildered face as he suddenly began racking his brain, trying to come up with an explanation for his arm dance and come up with it quick, before I could discover that he didn't actually have one. He had so much confidence that his mom, who knows pretty much everything, would know exactly what his gesture meant, that he hadn't bothered to invent a meaning for it. I said, "Billy. I think I know what your gesture means. It means 'I'm using my imagination'."

Billy was ecstatic with relief. "Yes, Mom! You're right! You knew it! You knew it!" Billy's reaction was loud and happy. I was happy too for coming up with the guess. We locked each other's arms into a gesture that didn't have to be practiced because we knew it so well. We embraced, and that gesture meant love.

Chapter 13

Attention!

- A typical child learns to recognize when he or she is required to pay attention and is able to focus his or her attention on a task for a reasonable length of time.

- The powerful gravity of Billy's subconscious mind is always pulling his attention inward. Even when I finally attract his attention, I have difficulty holding it on a task for any length of time.

- My task: to learn to maintain Billy's attention on a task for a reasonable time.

Every morning as our class begins, I make sure that Billy is aware of our location in time (Monday morning, for example) and in space (Aristotle School), of who I am (mom and teacher), what my task is in the school (to teach), and who he is (a sweet boy and student), and what is expected of him (to learn). Every morning we go through our stage-setting steps:

1. I pay homage to Billy's inner world by asking him if he has a story in the mirror of his mind (he always does) and then gently asking him to let go of it. Then I secure his compliance in participating in the class work by asking if he is ready to proceed.

2. We do the OM exercise to prepare his eyes to participate in the work as well.

3. We do our coordination exercises.

4. We bring all senses together, which means that we smile together, take a deep breath together and go through a routine of questions and answers which make clear whether I have his attention. If not, we repeat steps two and three until I do have his attention.

5. We "ground" Billy by making sure he has his weights on.

The stage is set. I've got his attention, and he is ready for me to teach him. Now we can go on with the show.

The first class is math. "Billy, today we will learn how to count by fives," I say, looking into his eyes. He is with me. "And now, look at the numbers on the board." I turn around, reach for my pointer, and prepare to go over the numbers on the board. I look at Billy. He is no longer with me.

I need to reconnect him to our class, and I'd better do it quickly. A quick reaction is important because, although I've lost Billy, so far I've lost only the train of his thoughts. They've just started to drift into some imagined world. In a little while they will organize themselves into meaningful associations; in another little while those associations will excite Billy. Then he'll start using them to create new, even more exciting images. After that it can be quite hard to pull him into the unexcitement of math. I'd have to go back and do at least some of the stage-setting steps, maybe all of them.

I didn't like losing Billy. Doing the stage-setting steps once is OK but doing them over is not. They take time, and the more time we spend on them, the less time is left for actual academic input. So I tried to come up with ideas about how not to lose him. Only two of my ideas turned out to be efficient tools to help keep Billy with me:

1. The art of asking questions.

2. The art of proving wrong.

The art of asking questions

(a) If I do the talking and expect Billy just to listen and make sense of my words, he'll probably stay with me for an average of three minutes before his attention starts drifting (that's assuming that what I have to say interests him).

(b) If Billy is doing an independent work, he'll stay with the task for an average of five minutes before his mind starts wandering (assuming that he has accepted his independent work rather than renouncing it).

0 1 2 3 4 5 6 7 8 9 0
0 1 2 3 4 5 6 7 8 9 0
0 1 2 3 4 5 6 7 8 9 0
0 1 2 3 4 5 6 7 8 9 0
0 1 2 3 4 5 6 7 8 9 0
0 1 2 3 4 5 6 7 8 9 0
0 1 2 3 4 5 6 7 8 9 0
0 1 2 3 4 5 6 7 8 9 0
0 1 2 3 4 5 6 7 8 9 0

However, if during (a) or (b) I insert a number of questions, then these questions serve as an interlocking mechanism that together with (a) or (b) can hold his brain for a long time – as long as 30 to 45 minutes. Raising questions is like ordering more and more things in a restaurant just to be able to keep your table and not be kicked out of the house. Before the table is empty, make another order. Before Billy's attention exhausts itself, raise another question.

The questions certainly cannot be arbitrary. They should be related in one way or another to the task in which the student is engaged. A question should support (gently) the specific study process rather than disrupt it. For example, Billy's assignment is to read several sentences aloud. He interrupts himself with a joke about monsters that just came to his mind. Before his joke distracts both of us, I quickly ask him a question such as "Sorry, I missed the end of your last sentence, what was it?" or "How many sentences did you read so far?" or "Look at the next sentence. Is the first word too hard for you?"

If Billy insists on telling the joke, I remark gently that I will listen to the joke at break time. Then I repeat the question. Ninety-nine percent of the time, the question will arrest his attention, and his desire to come up with a correct answer will bring him back to his assignment. Simple directions such as "Keep reading," "Don't interrupt," or "Pay attention" do not work with Billy. He sees them as invitations to resist; they're a quick way to lose him completely.

Now every time I have to turn around to reach for some teaching supplies, or if have to write something on the board, I make sure that I fill in this time with questions. Depending on the class, they might be something like these.

"What number comes after 63?"

"A pizza has 12 slices. You eat half. How many slices did you leave for your sister?"

"Can you count by fives for me?"

"What is a noun? Maybe it's a bird?"

"What is a verb? Maybe a pumpkin?"

"The word 'cloud' – is it a noun or a verb?"

"How do you spell 'black'?"

The magic of this tool is simple. When Billy gets the answer right, he feels like a winner. Winning makes the brain release a chemical (or more than one?) which we perceive as pleasurable. Winning makes us feel good. Every time we pass a test, we feel good. Every time we get an answer right, we feel good. In comparison with *The Wheel Of Fortune*, Billy's prize for winning (inner satisfaction) is an intangible piece of nothing. Yet the effect on his brain is much the same.

This principle of accessing the pleasure center of the brain is also at the core of tool number two for fixing Billy's attention on a task.

The art of proving wrong

I have yet to meet anyone who does not delight, at some point in their earthly life, in proving someone wrong. Oh, how delightful is the awareness of being right, especially at the expense of someone else being wrong! 'Oh, how reassuring, how exalting!' Billy thinks so too.

"Billy, six plus two is nine, right?" It takes him about fifteen seconds to figure out that I'm wrong. He corrects me with an authority worthy of a professor and a triumph worthy of a warrior.

"No, it's not! You got it wrong, Mom! It's eight! See now?"

"Oh," I say, "how could I possibly think that? Thanks for setting me straight."

Billy is fond of correcting a list of synonyms or antonyms: "Mom, messy is not the opposite of dirty! That's wrong! The right answer should be clean!"

He likes correcting any simple arithmetic. He also works gladly with lists of words given to him for proofreading. It may happen that a number of malicious mistakes creep into the lists. Billy is the one to discover the intruders who defile the English language. He finds them all right, and I express my sincere gratitude for his help. We're happy, both of us. He's happy because correcting errors made him feel good; I'm happy because he feels good and because I succeeded in keeping his subconscious mind within the boundaries of our classroom.

A class filled with many questions answered and many errors caught is always a good class. After such a class Billy often comments, "Mom, we had such good fun! I liked this class very much!"

PART III
A Teacher's Strategies

The Church

I saw the church. The church is a wonderful place.

I bet there were more than 50 angels on the gold altar.

I learned that everyone who was here worked on it.

I thought that it must have taken a humongous amount of time to put together.

We were very quiet because you cannot talk in the Church.

Chapter 14

Connecting the world

> - A typical child comprehends intuitively what is going on in a vast majority of the social scenes that happen around him.
>
> - Billy is not able to understand the social world on his own.
>
> - My task: to learn to connect the dots for Billy so that he can comprehend the patterns of social events.

In the Aristotle School, our classes started at 9:15 A.M. Before that, Billy and I would drive Francesca to Loma Portal Elementary, where the bell rang at 8:40 A.M. We would park the car as close to the school as we could, then walk with Francesca to the school field. Knowing Francesca's shyness, if no one she knew well was there I'd hang around for a little while until a friend of hers arrived to keep her company.

The time on the field was a trial for me. While I tried to stay with my daughter and give her encouragement for the day, my son would repeatedly escape my close supervision and push, punch, bother or annoy one child or another. When that happened, which was often, I'd get mad. I'd go after Billy, grab his hand and flee the field, filled with yearning for the uneventful, calm mornings that a mother tending to her two lovely children should have. I'd take Billy back to the car, reminding him of his promises to stay with me and Francesca. I always made an effort to stay cool, not to let the morning's incidents throw me off balance.

One morning, though, I did go off balance. Billy was rowdy on the field. When I tried to get him to leave, he ran away from me, and I had to chase him.

Once I'd caught him, I pushed him ahead of me so we could leave the school grounds faster. Billy didn't move fast enough, and, in my off-state, I came up with nothing better than to push my little boy's behind with my foot, which was sporting a black shiny boot. Needless to say, Billy didn't like that, but it made him move faster and away from the school. At home we talked about it. I apologized and asked him (again) not to bother the children any more. He promised (again) not to. We forgave each other, hugged, put the incident behind us and proceeded with the day.

The incident, though, did not dissolve into another blurred image of the past. As I was to find out that afternoon when I went to school to get Francesca, what had happened on the field had already crept its way into the future because someone on the field saw me "kicking my child with my boot" and reported that to the principal. I was summoned to the principal's office to give an explanation.

I gave one. I said that I was a mother doing a full-time job with an autistic child. That sometimes I am drained emotionally. That yes, it might have looked like I kicked Billy, but it was only a pretend kick. It was supposed to alert him rather than cause him physical pain. That I really, really did not hurt him. That, of course, it was not wise to do that. That I'm sorry. I wished I could turn things around and not have done it. But there I was, as helpless to change the past as I was to control my boy.

The principal listened to me. She watched me fight my tears and then be unable to fight them anymore. With disarming compassion, she said, "Yours is a hard job. I understand." Ashamed and humiliated, I left. For several weeks after that, my life was filled with misery, a misery that made it hard to drink, to eat, or to breathe. I felt devastating guilt for my deed – not because I had hurt Billy, for I knew that I hadn't – but from knowing that I had been out of control. If I had been in charge of my emotions at the time, I would not have kicked Billy, however lightly. I would have known better.

During those weeks of misery, I did everything I was supposed to do. I shopped, cooked, cleaned, ironed, taught, helped with homework, made beds, fetched night-time snacks and made sure that I looked good. As for my black shiny boots, I put them out of sight, but I could not put away the misery that clung to my soul.

A few weeks later I happened to take part in group meditation with some people I knew. Our group leader asked all of us to "put our names in the circle" – to speak our names in turn as a means of offering something to the group. We did, and then we closed our eyes and relaxed. We were invited to let a question surface in our minds, a question which was important to us. From there we were to slide into the stillness of our minds, where answers were to be found.

My question surfaced immediately. "God, how do I find peace for my soul?" In the stillness of my mind I knelt and laid in front of me all my guilt, my misery, my desire to be strong enough never again to go off balance. Then it became all dark. My spirit was lifted far, far into the darkness. I moved swiftly in a dark space, away from the Earth, as if I needed to cover a distance as great as my suffering. At some point, my movement stopped. In my meditative dream, in that darkness, there was a free-floating tower with innumerable openings. From those openings, as if from a beehive, a humming sound was spreading into space. I let its vibrations penetrate my spirit, and suddenly I sensed that my misery was lifted by that sound. The weight that I'd been carrying was there no longer. I listened to the humming sound and to the peace in my soul, and it was beautiful.

Suddenly, I saw the Earth. I felt a need to shift my eyes, and soon, far down, I saw San Diego, and then Loma Portal Elementary. The dream went on, taking me closer to the ground, and I saw, from a bird's height, the school field in the morning. I saw how the teacher on duty on the field directed the children into lines, each class forming a line of its own. The lines were like the threads of a net, catching the children and moving them into the places where they belonged. And I saw Billy. My little Billy, who ran between the lines, bumping into everybody and disrupting the net of the lines. Billy had no place for himself, and so, as if moved by an outside force, he oscillated from line to line, causing disorder.

As I watched him, a question came to me suddenly. What if Billy didn't know why the children went to the field in the morning? What if he was not aware of the lines? I had never explained to Francesca the purpose of being on the field in the mornings. I had never needed to. She knew why, just as the other children knew why. I realized that I'd been assuming that Billy too knew why. But what if my assumption about Billy was wrong? What if he had no clue about the social nets around him? Then he could not be aware that he was disrupting a net. What if?

The next morning, in the Aristotle School, we talked about the school field and what Billy told me was most enlightening.

Mom: Billy, why do you think the children gather on the school field in the mornings? You know, like when we take Francesca to school?

Billy: I don't know.

Mom: Well, take a guess. What do you think they are supposed to do there?

Billy: I guess…maybe, play?

Mom: So, it's your guess that they gather there to play?

Billy: Yes. To play and to have fun!

The vision of my meditative dream was accurate. Billy did not know what was going on out there on the field. And I understood then that there could be many, many other situations in which I had just assumed that Billy understood the social basis of human interactions. I winced at the idea that I had to reevaluate all of Billy's misbehaviors. But I could no longer write Billy off as refractory until I was sure that he knew all the rules of the social nets around him.

The task I was facing was the need for me to chew up reality for Billy. (In my homeland, where there was no commercial baby food, mothers chew the food for their tiny babies.) Although he had long passed the age when he was supposed to masticate social scenes for himself, he still lacked the teeth for it. While I wasn't thrilled about the size of the job ahead of us, I knew that I had learned an important lesson about Billy. Suddenly the incident on the school field made sense, and my subsequent misery did too. I felt as if I had come full circle. There was a purpose in what had happened, and that purpose was a lesson. Once I'd learned the lesson, the misery left me.

Net Fixers

As time went on, I brought my black shiny boots out of hiding. Once again I felt good wearing them. But I kept thinking very, very hard about teaching Billy how to connect the dots of the world around him, how to understand the intersections of human behavior and recognize their patterns. From that I conceived Net Fixers, which later came to play a great role in my guiding Billy along the paths of our intricate world. Our first Net Fixer was The School Field.

The school field

Mom: Billy, look here. This is the school, here are the bungalows. When the bell rings, the children go to their classes, yes?

Billy: Yes.

Mom: Do all the children go to the same bungalow?

Billy: No.

Mom: Do they go to different bungalows?

Billy: Yes!

Mom: You are very right. The children go to different bungalows. But do they choose any bungalow they want?

Billy: No!

Mom: How do they know where to go?

Billy: Because. They go to their class, you know.

Mom: But first they gather in the field, right?

Billy: Right.

Mom: Now let's draw a picture of the field, there.

Billy: The playground is here.

Mom: OK, let's draw the playground. And now I'm going to draw the children. See, I'm making these lines on the field. Do you know why?

Billy: Why?

Mom: Because in the morning the children come to the field not to play. They come to stay in lines.

Billy: Why?

Mom: Because the children come right before the bell rings. Then the teachers come to take the children to different classes. If the children were playing, how would every teacher find the children of his or her class? It would be a mess!

Billy: A mess! So they can't play?

Mom: No. The children, in the morning, should find the line for their class and wait nicely for their teacher. But they could come and play on the field at the recess time, right?

Billy: Right. I like to play tag at recess.

Mom: Tag is OK. But not in the mornings. Only at recess time. Do you understand?

Billy: Yes, I understand now.

Mom: Cool. Now let's draw lines which will show the way for each line to go to different classes with their teacher. When the children leave, the school field would become empty. The children would be learning. And we would be learning at our Aristotle School. OK?

Billy: OK.

People who've worked with autistic children are familiar with Social Stories. Social Stories are designed to teach children about social scenes, and they have the same goals as my Net Fixers. But while I've used Social Stories with Billy, with some success, I've had better results from Net Fixers. How are Net Fixers different from Social Stories?

1. A Net Fixer is created in the presence of the child and with his active participation in the process of creation. When we read Social Stories, Billy remained merely a witness, but he was a participant in the Net Fixers.

2. The Net Fixer is created as a series of questions, designed in such a way that the child's answers lead him to understanding a social situation.

3. The Net Fixer is created visually as much as logically. The child is not asked to look at pictures which someone else has already drawn. The magic of creation happens in front of his eyes, capturing his attention and helping him make the connections for himself.

Whenever I introduce Billy to a new Net Fixer, I invite him to sit on a stool next to me by the board. We are not teacher and student anymore. We are equals. As I ask questions and create the picture, I coax him to participate. I might ask him if my picture needs fixing, or if he thinks that we should add some details to it. His participation is valuable. Like a magnet, it attracts his mind to the story and holds it there.

Watching how Billy benefited from our Net Fixers, I was envious. I wished I had someone in my life to connect the dots of the world for me. I thought of the places I've lived and the people I've met. As I drifted into the past, I made brief stops to gaze at moments when I did something that wasn't quite right and which made me feel utterly inadequate. From the distance, I could easily see that my missteps happened not because I was stupid, but because I didn't have a good understanding of a particular social net.

My childhood came to mind. My father's job required us to move several times, from village to village. In each new village I'd be thrown into a pool of children who were entangled in an invisible net of interrelationships woven by families living in the same place for many, many generations. I was not related to any of them. I was the new manager's offspring. The children's interactions at school were a reflection of their interactions outside school. I was not a part of their lives outside school and I did not fit in.

In one of the villages I lived in, there was an orphanage. Eighteen orphanage children were in my grade, enough to form a class of their own. Tired of being inadequate among the village children, I went to the principal and asked to be moved to the class of orphanage children. The principal granted my wish, and I felt very fortunate. The orphanage kids were not related to each other. Each came with a different story, but they were alike in one way: the orphanage children's interaction with reality was one of survival. They all looked at the world with one eye sad and the other full of hope. I could relate to that. I stayed in that class.

Later, I did not fit anywhere in the whole communist net of the Soviet Union. When a KGB officer told me to "leave the country or else" I chose to leave. I left Russia on a very cold February day, in an Aeroflot plane with only four other passengers on board. In Europe, thanks to my status of political refugee, I had several options in choosing a new country of residence. I chose the United States. England and Holland, which were other options, seemed to me just like those villages of my childhood in which I felt so inadequate. The United States though, was a country of orphans. It gathered orphans from all over the world, and they came to this promised land with one eye full of sadness and the other full of hope. I could relate to that, and I found it to be true: the spirit of America is acceptance. As long as I'm careful to correct my vocabulary to the demands of time, I'm fine. If, in addition to that, I have my legs shaved and drive below the speed limit, I feel totally, absolutely adequate.

As I got older, I kept learning from my own mistakes, but I don't care much for that kind of learning. The Net Fixers would have suited me better. If someone had been drawing pictures for me, showing me the rules of different social games, maybe I could have avoided my inadequacies altogether. I remembered all the times when my immigrant friends felt inadequate. They too could have used a Net Fixer here and there.

Connecting reality is hard, and not only for Billy. His exaggerated disconnectedness is a reminder of our own disconnectedness. So often we're lost although we are perfectly typical unautistic adults, even with diplomas to attest to the quality of our minds. But just like Billy, we're sometimes at a loss because we fail to make the right connections in social reality.

Once in a while I close my eyes and let myself go into the stillness of a far-away dark space and listen to the humming from the tower. There, I connect my children's misbehaviors with my own inadequacies and sacrifice them all to the gods. Let there be more free space in our souls, so we can connect with the spirit.

Chapter 15

On acquiring knowledge

- A typical child knows that he goes to school to learn.

- Billy went to school to have fun. Learning was an unwanted extra activity.

- My task: to teach Billy to have fun learning.

When Billy was in Theresa's class, she forced him to do things for her. She made him finish his projects whether he wanted or not. Firm and loving, she knew the art of combining discipline with gentleness. But as we learned for ourselves, maintaining discipline with an autistic child was not as easy as it seemed when watching Theresa.

In other teachers' classes, discipline was applied in moderation. Billy was taught only when he accepted it. If he refused to learn, the assistant took him for a walk. At other times Billy bargained for some carpet time for himself (i.e., to sit on the classroom carpet and read a book of his own choosing). His teachers, in their turn, didn't hesitate to use treats to encourage him to learn. Billy learned to expect the easy life.

When I started homeschooling Billy, I knew I'd have to deal with his expectation that he could take things easy, but take it easy I could not. There was no time to lose. We were losing his young years, those most fertile for success in altering autistic traits. Our Aristotle School could succeed only if Billy could be forced (although in a gentle way) to acquire knowledge.

There was the easy way, the way of tempting him with a Coke or a lollipop in exchange for an effort at learning; but that method didn't seem to live up to the name of our school. Temptation is a powerful emotion, but I wanted to have Billy enticed into learning not by appeals to his taste buds but by the pleasure of learning itself.

Our first weeks in the Aristotle School were weeks of an unfair division of labor. My labor, the teacher's, was enforcement. Billy's labor, as the student, was defense. That had to change. I wanted us to be united, and unite we did. A Net Fixer helped: What is knowledge for?

What is knowledge for?

Mom: What is knowledge for, Billy?

Billy: I don't know.

Mom: Let's see. When a person knows lots and lots of things, what do we call that person?

Billy: Smart?

Mom: Yes! You've got it! When a person knows a lot, we say, "What a smart person!"

Billy: I'm *very* smart.

Mom: You sure are. You are six years old smart, right?

Billy: Right.

Mom: What about Daddy? Do you think he is also six years old smart? Or does he know much more?

Billy: He knows lots and lots.

Mom: More than you?

Billy: Yes!

Mom: But why do you think Daddy knows lots more than you do?

Billy: M-m-m-m…

Mom: It's because he has a lot of knowledge in his brain. Right?

Billy: Daddy has a big brain!

Mom: But how did that knowledge get into his brain? Did he become smart because he ate a banana?

Billy: No! You don't get smart from bananas, Mom!

Mom: You're right. Not from bananas. How about watermelons? Do you get smart from watermelons?

Billy: This is silly, Mom!

Mom: Maybe he is smart because he reads a lot of books and learns about things?

Billy: Yes, that's how.

Mom: What about you? Would you like to be a big man like Daddy and still be only six years old smart?

Billy: No! I want to be very, very smart like Daddy.

Mom: But if you want to get smarter and smarter, that means you have to learn lots and lots, right?

Billy: Yes, Mom! I want to learn lots and lots and be very, very smart. I want to be the smartest of all! You're going to teach me how to be the smartest of all, Mom?

Mom: I sure am. But that means we need to learn subtraction, and all the short and long vowels, and how to tell time and lots of other things.

Billy: [Sighs] Yes, I know.

Mom: Billy, we could make learning those thing lots of fun. It's fun to learn when you know that you're getting smarter. I mean, if you don't want to learn, we could close our school, and you could play a lot and stay six years old smart.

Billy: No! I want to learn!

By the end of the Net Fixer, Billy was through with the propaganda and was ready to go on and learn something. Our roles changed from that of enforcement versus defense to a common effort to make Billy smart. Billy's attitude toward learning became one of acquiring wealth. Little by little he was getting richer and richer in knowledge.

Subsequently it became very important that we stated, at the end of every class, what exactly we had learned. Sometimes we didn't learn much. Some days Billy wasn't quite present, and there was a lot of lost time. But when we had a class of joyful learning, Billy would jump up from his chair and yell, with great enthusiasm, "Mom, that was such a good class! I know so, so much now!"

Billy started taking great pride in showing off his knowledge. His father withstood a daily dosage of bragging about vowels or proper nouns – not that he minded.

Wild Poem

The pink turtle wore a tutu
Red lips locked a great sweet kiss
The angry lion had a face like death
The chattering teeth chattered through the night
The magic wand flashed its power

Billy

Chapter 16

Remember?

> - A typical child knows how to remember things. Sometimes he may remember better than his parents.
>
> - Billy needed to be taught how to remember.
>
> - My task: to teach Billy to store information in his mind and to be able to recall that information.

One of the hardships in teaching Billy was the difficulty with which new information settled in his brain. In the beginning I often lost patience because Billy could not remember what I had taught him the day before. But one day I realized how impatient his inability to retain information made me, and I found myself laughing hysterically at the thought of an impatient person teaching an autistic child; it's like having Khrushchev teach diplomacy. Sometimes I was really close to taking my shoe off and pounding it on Billy's desk.

So the time came when I had to tell my impatience goodbye. Billy was what he was. He was atypical. His capacity to memorize was atypical too. I needed to observe him, establish his personal patterns of memorizing and be guided in my teaching by those patterns. I thought of a memory as a picture built up in the brain by layers of new information. Each repetition of a specific bit of information puts down an additional layer on the same picture in the brain. Francesca, for example, needed about two layers of repetition to memorize simple things. When it came to poems, she needed about five layers of repetition.

Billy's memorizing pattern was different from Francesca's. For every one of her layers, he needed about five. So we started to take time to repeat any new word, any new knowledge, many times. We made as many layers in the brain as were needed until the information settled in for good. Some things Billy could memorize in one day, but more often than not I had to keep track of what was being memorized and reinforce it several days in a row. Billy's memorizing was also helped by making him aware of his memory and its magic.

We have a mirror in our brain

Mom: Billy, look. This is a new word. It means to be kind.

Billy: Ge-ne-rous.

Mom: Now close your eyes and say it with your eyes closed.

Billy: M-m. Mom, let me look one more time.

Mom: OK, look one more time. [Billy looks at the board, then closes his eyes again.]

Billy: Generous.

Mom: Good! How did you remember it?

Billy: Because. It was in my brain.

Mom: That's right. There's a mirror in our minds. When the mirror of your mind had the word generous in it, you could just close your eyes and find it there.

Billy: I know. I can close my eyes and find it there.

Mom: OK. Now read this poem.

Billy: Teddy Bear, Teddy Bear, turn around.
Teddy Bear, Teddy Bear, touch the ground.
Teddy Bear, Teddy Bear, show your shoe.
Teddy Bear, Teddy Bear, that will do.

Mom: Now close your eyes. Say the teddy bear poem.

Billy: Teddy Bear, Teddy Bear, I can't remember.

Mom: Oops. What happened? When you read this word – generous – you closed your eyes and said it right away. But not the poem?

Billy: The poem is hard, Mom.

Mom: Yes, the poem is hard. Close your eyes. Look in the mirror of your mind. Is it there?

Billy: It's not.

Mom: But see, one word is very short. You said it only two times, and it was in the mirror of your mind. You could remember it. But the poem is longer. I think we need to say it several times until it will settle in the mirror of your mind.

Billy: Yeah.

Mom: Let's try to find out how many times we need to say the poem before it goes into the mirror of your mind.

Billy: OK.

It took about seven repetitions before Billy could say the poem. Every time he thought he knew it, I'd ask him to close his eyes and see if the poem was in the mirror of his mind and say it with his eyes closed. If there were pieces missing from the picture of the poem, we filled them in until Billy could say the poem in one breath.

He became very fond of learning poems and then reciting them to whoever was around, whether they wanted to listen or not. Our guests who had to endure Billy's recitations did it in a way which I should describe with Billy's new word – generous. That means to be kind.

As I taught Billy I learned more about the specifics of his patterns of memorizing. As we memorize, the information is stored in blocks. There is one for addition, one for vowels, one for days of the week and one for months of the year. For Billy it was very difficult, and still is, to shift from one block of memory into another. Sometimes I'd ask him a simple question such as, "What is a proper noun?" and he'd answer "I don't know." I knew, though, that the

answer was in the mirror of his mind. Billy just couldn't access that answer. The solution was to build an association that led him to the correct block of information in his brain – in this case, the block which held information about nouns.

Mom: Billy, what are nouns? I think they are some kind of goat.

Billy: No, Mom! They're not goats!

Mom: No? Maybe not. Then maybe they're porcupines.

Billy: Mom!

Mom: Well, what are they then? Maybe some kind of words?

Billy: Yes, they are words.

Mom: What kind of words?

Billy: Words that name things.

Mom: Right! And what kinds of nouns do we know?

Billy: There are proper nouns.

Mom: Yes, there are. Which are those?

Billy: Billy. Nebraska. Names of pets. Right?

Mom: Right you are.

Since I left the house of my parents at the age of 16 for university, I've rarely spoken the Romanian language. When I have to speak it, I feel at first as if the part of my brain containing Romanian has gone numb, like a leg that's gone to sleep after a long time sitting on it. Flex it a bit, and it's as good as new.

My first few hours of speaking Romanian are definitely not a good indicator of my overall mastery of it. After two or three hours, I become almost as fluent in Romanian as I was 30 years ago. I think that the information retrieval system in Billy's brain goes to sleep at a much faster rate than average. The blocks of his brain need to be flexed repeatedly to remain accessible. Therefore his performance on tests, if they are administered to him in the same way as to a typical child, will not be an accurate reflection of his knowledge. A test is more objective if dedicated to one subject at a time and Billy has an opportunity to flex that block of his brain before the test.

It has been rewarding to see that Billy's brain is not completely rigid but actually changes as he learns more and more. I've seen that the larger a block of knowledge becomes and the more associations we build, the easier it becomes for Billy to access that knowledge. Billy will enter manhood with a combination of his inherited abilities plus the sum of what he can remember. How he relates to the world will depend on what he can see in the mirror of his mind. When faced with challenges, Billy will close his eyes and look into that mirror for solutions.

I'm sure we'll succeed in committing to Billy's memory enough English and math for him to be able to make his own way in the world. But besides that, should I attempt to place in the mirror of his mind a block for self-doubt, a block for self-confidence, a block for being open with people, another for keeping his own secrets? Teaching takes on a different dimension when there is an awareness that what we are layering in the child's brain will become a part of him for the rest of his life. A teacher is but a master maker of memories. Better be a skillful one.

Chapter 17

The five-senses approach

- A typical child is taught as a whole entity.

- Billy has to be divided into parts – ears, eyes, nose, tongue, and muscles – and each part has to be taught separately.

- My task: to spread knowledge across Billy's senses until we find the one by which he learns most efficiently.

When I was a student in the schools of the Soviet Union, my teachers made extensive use of the blackboard as a teaching tool. My association of the classroom with a usable board is so strong that I'm always startled in the classrooms of my children's schools in San Diego when I see the boards covered with posters or blocked, as if barricaded, by shelves and desks. My daughter has been in public schools for six years now, and not once has she been asked to work at the board.

As for me, I could close my eyes and drift into my sixth grade. My math teacher was Paraskoviya Konstantinovna, a petite woman with a long braid. A touch of sadness still clung to her appearance, from her childhood in an orphanage. In her youth, algebra and geometry had been her substitutes for a family, and she still loved her subjects with deep devotion, and loved children who loved her subjects. Going to her math class was special. It was beauty and discovery, savoring reacquaintance with old knowledge and anticipating the thrill of the new.

Paraskoviya Konstantinovna wore the same skirt all year round; she was the most poorly dressed teacher I ever saw. Thin, she looked like a little girl running among the traditional three rows of desks in our classroom. She kept an algebra book at her chest and a pen in her mouth. The kids hid their giggles at seeing her colored mouth, blue from the ink running from her pen. "And now," she'd turn around in search for the next victim, "Olga, you go to the board."

Many kids hated going to the board but I loved it. My sense of responsibility and of living up to Paraskoviya Konstantinovna's expectations lifted me from my chair and transported me to the board, chalk in one hand, a damp rag in the other. In a moment she'd be dictating a problem to me, and I knew it would be a difficult one. But somehow when I was at the board and filled with desire to please my teacher, I knew more than I knew I knew. My brain acquired a sharp edge to it; it worked fast and figured things out almost effortlessly.

That was to become my best way of learning – one of responsibility, one of love for my teacher or a subject. Whatever I learned in a state of indifference seemed to make its way into my stomach and down rather than going into my brain. But brought into a state of emotional involvement, with noble reasons for my learning, I learned fast.

There are people who need to write things down if they want to learn them. There are people who learn while listening to heavy metal music. Some need to listen to a lecture on earphones. There are those who learn best in libraries and others who lock themselves away from all living souls. My sister learned only what entered her brain through her right ear. The hearing of her left ear was impaired. And there was Tamara, a young woman at my university, who believed that if she was to pass an exam she needed to sleep the night before with the books under her pillow.

With so many ways to organize a learning process, how was I, a new teacher, to choose the best for my son? I had no special knowledge about the five basic human senses (hearing, seeing, touch and movement, taste and smell) and their connection with the brain and learning; how was I to make sure that I didn't miss some valuable teaching methods? And how about establishing the dominance of the left and right sides of the brain? It would have been wonderful to have had time to educate myself in matters of the mind. I did try, but with my time limits it was a slow education. So I resolved to just use what I already knew and to keep learning.

No device existed that could analyze Billy and give me a printout of his dominant learning pathways and how to use them. Therefore, in my teaching I had to bombard all his senses with knowledge, and see what worked and what didn't. We checked Billy's hearing. At the time he couldn't talk, at four, and we suspected that his hearing might be responsible. It wasn't. But just in case there was some undetected deficiency in one of his ears I decided that in class I was going to stand right in front of him.

I have a hard time relating to the way children are seated in many school classrooms these days – six to eight children sitting around a table, facing each other. This type of arrangement is disastrous for Billy. He would rather make funny faces at other kids than look at the teacher, and in this arrangement, nothing forces him to look at the teacher. In fact, everything forces him to look at the other kids. While the teacher drifts through the classroom, the children have to keep craning their necks to locate her.

I decided I was going to stand right in front of Billy, like the Statue of Liberty in front of New York, to make sure he need not crane his neck to locate me. This was the first step in my five-senses approach to teaching. I called this one "centering."

The second step was to go to a music store and buy a large, impressive xylophone. Billy likes big things, and I wanted him to like the xylophone. The xylophone was to support the stimulation of Billy's audio perception of the world. We played the xylophone every time Billy had a hard time pronouncing an English word, for while he labored at saying some words, he had no trouble singing them.

I must admit that I have no musical education whatsoever. I don't even have a good ear so I save my singing for times when I'm driving alone on the highway. Nevertheless, I sang with Billy. I'd choose a little tune – me-fa-sol-sol-me-fa-sol-sol – and sing a word along with it: "Pa-ra-graph-one-Pa-ra-graph-two." Billy was very tolerant of my singing. Sometimes I thought he even liked it.

We also sang any new definition. After we had repeated several times "A verb is an action word," we'd sing the definition, our xylophone struggling together with our voices. Billy often took over the xylophone, loving the magic of evoking sounds from the bright metal plates.

The third step was to incorporate board work into the class. I pretended I was Paraskoviya Konstantinovna.

"And now," I'd pause, searching through my one-student class, "to the board will go…"

"Me, me! I'll go to the board!" Billy eagerly thrust his arm skyward.

"All right, then. Billy Holland. Go to the board. On the left side of the board write three common nouns. On the right side three proper nouns. You may choose markers of different colors for the left and the right sides."

"I'd like green for the left side. And red for the other one. It's going to look great!" And Billy would do his board work, filled with desire to please me.

Thus, we addressed both his visual perception and his motor perception and got him emotionally involved as well.

It was interesting that none of Billy's senses was dominant. Sometimes singing was very important, sometimes drawing was important. When I taught English, we relied on a combination of audio, visual and motor senses. But math concepts were hard for Billy. When I taught math, I had to create a setting in which all five senses were involved, smell and taste along with the other three. How to do it? We had pretend parties, with Billy as planner. We served pretend foods which smelled and tasted good: "M-m-m, yummy pizza! How does it smell? Good? How does it taste? Good? How many pieces would you serve to your guests? Three pieces each? So how many pieces do we need altogether?" Or we'd have a pretend garden with many beautiful flowers with gorgeous smells. We'd add tulips to roses to carnations. All our parties involved "pretend" sensations, not real ones, for two reasons: to train Billy's abstract thinking, and to keep "treats" out of the classroom.

The more of Billy's senses that become involved in his learning, the better are the results. I love coming up with new ideas, such as saying a hard word while standing on the left foot, and then while standing on the right foot; or learning to say something the way a cowboy would; or to write a word as a ballerina would. She'd write small, graceful letters, all of them above the lines and all of them just the right size, wouldn't she?

"Billy, would you please give me the gift of small, beautiful letters?"

"Sure, Mom," says Billy. On the wave of the emotion of giving a gift, his letters, for a line or two, are indeed as precise as if written by a ballerina. But then the ballerina image fades, and Billy's letters drift below the lines and straggle across the page. And I watch him, wondering if it's a good time to ask for another gift of beautiful writing, or for now just leave him to his effort.

As I wonder, I feel overwhelmed by a sense of gratitude. The older I get, the more grateful I become, and the less my gratefulness is identified with anything in particular. I'm just grateful to tears.

3-27-01

Billy

Write each word 2 times. underline <u>au</u> and <u>aw</u>

1	cr<u>aw</u>l	crawl	crawl
2	<u>au</u>to	auto	auto
3	l<u>au</u>ndry	laundry	laundry
4	h<u>aw</u>k	hawk	hawk
5	s<u>au</u>ce	sauce	sauce
6	f<u>au</u>cet	faucet	faucet
7	sh<u>aw</u>l	shawl	shawl
8	c<u>au</u>ght	caught	caught
9	dr<u>aw</u>	draw	draw
10	y<u>aw</u>n	yawn	yah yawn
11	l<u>aw</u>n	lawn	lawn
12	str<u>aw</u>	straw	straw
13	p<u>aw</u>s	paws	paws
14	l<u>aw</u>s	laws	laws
15	dr<u>aw</u>er	drawer	draw draw
16	dr<u>aw</u>ing	drawing	draing
17	r<u>aw</u>	raw	raw
18	s<u>au</u>cer	saucer	sauer
19	s<u>au</u>sage	sausage	sausage

Chapter 18

English as a step-language

> • A typical child learns a language simply by being consciously alert to the surrounding world, by observing it and by being a copy-cat.
>
> • Billy, mostly, is not consciously alert to the surrounding world. His observational skills are very limited.
>
> • My task: to teach new words to Billy.

I was born in a republic of the former USSR. The people of my village, and most of the other villages where I lived when I was growing up, spoke the Romanian language. When I was three my father was assigned to work in a Russian-speaking town. There I learned the Russian language, although I have no memory of learning it: I just know that I know it. I know it better than Romanian, even though Romanian was the language of our home.

I was drawn to the sound of Russian as far back as I can remember. At six I implored my parents to send me to a Russian school, but my mother was firm in having me learn the language of my motherland, which was Romanian. Obediently, I went to a school that taught in Romanian; but I kept my Russian world with me. I read in Russian, I spent my summers in camps with Russian children.

In Russian I was not the person I was in Romanian. In Romanian, I was the child educated by her parents and the village, with reactions and responses which were perfectly adequate by the village's standards. In Russian, though, I was an altogether different child. I kept my inner world in Russian, and in that world I was different from the people around me. My Russian thoughts merged with Russian fairy tales and stories. As I tended chicks and ducklings and worked in the garden, I'd slip into my Russian world and become a warrior, a KGB spy or a seeker of wonders. Inner or outer, a Russian world had to be dramatic and tragic. And my inner world was.

Later in my life, the pull of the Russian language overtook my ties to my motherland. I went to a university that taught in Russian. I married a Russian man and moved to Moscow. There, for the first time in my life, I experienced what I thought was true happiness. Walking in busy Russian crowds, scouting bookstores full of Russian books, having Russian friends – it all was a dream come true. I felt that I had been starved for the Russian language, starved with my entire body and for a long time. I couldn't have enough of it. I didn't care that Moscow was cold and dark for months on end, unlike my warm-weathered, pleasant motherland. Snow or no snow, clouds or more clouds, Moscow was constantly filled with the magnificent murmur of a language in which every cell of my body bathed in comfort.

Whenever I visited my homeland and my parent's house, where I had to speak Romanian, I became stiff. My sense of comfort vanished, leaving an emptiness that only a conscious effort of my body could fill with Romanian. But my body resisted the adjustment, and a week-long visit would end in an inner exhaustion that only the Russian murmur of the Moscow streets could cure.

When, later in my life, I examined my affair with the Russian language, I came to these conclusions: I realized that I functioned differently in Russian than in Romanian. I cultivated different habits and reactions in Russian than the ones I had learned in Romanian. I liked myself better in Russian. In Russian I felt smarter, I felt more intelligent. I was more likely to be reasonable in Russian, less likely to indulge in anger or despair. My laughter came more easily in Russian. My Russian tears were of a different chemistry than my Romanian tears. I didn't mind the Russian ones; I couldn't stand the Romanian. The Russian language seemed, somehow, to bring me comfort on a very physical level. It felt like a wonderfully comfortable coat, a coat which every single cell of my body could relax in. So my bilingual upbringing brought interesting results. While the Romanian language was my mother tongue, Russian was my favorite. It became my chosen language.

I don't remember when I realized that Billy had a chosen language of his own. It was a slow realization, one that came from observing Billy at his happy moments, when he'd make odd motions and noises, when he'd screech, yell, or utter some strange combinations of sound. Somehow I *saw* how much comfort he had with himself when he was in his inner world, even though it operated in a language that sounded so weird to us. I thought maybe it sounded weird only because it wasn't English, or Russian, or Romanian.

What was Billy's chosen language; the one that was to him deeply familiar, instantly recognized; the one that conditioned his strange behavior? I wished I knew. I wished I could recognize it. Then I could try to learn it myself. Then maybe I could speak it, and maybe we would understand each other so well. But I only caught, here and there, little waves of sounds and images that I was guessing must be in his chosen language.

I'm only now learning not to be afraid of the oddity of that tongue of his, so unlike any I've heard in my life; so unearthly, or so unlike what I've learned to perceive as earthly. Sometimes, when I catch waves of sounds and images of his chosen language, I feel a jolt of helplessness that blocks my judgment; and from that place of non-judgment I suddenly perceive Billy's chosen language as hauntingly beautiful and mysterious. But those are only moments. Sadly, there are still times when I can't help overruling Billy's noises as annoying and unacceptable.

It was a fortunate guess that Billy had a chosen language of his own for it meant that English comes to him, actually, as a second language. While I was at great odds with the notion of teaching language to a child who cannot speak any language at all, I was much more comfortable teaching English as a second language to someone who already knew how to speak in something. I knew how to teach English as a second language.

I came to the United States in 1986, seven years before Billy's birth. I came armed with the English vocabulary of my dissident past in Moscow, a vocabulary which allowed me to inform a reporter about an arrest or a hunger strike, but not much else. And my then-English was all in the present tense. It had no concept of time or space. While it served me in my dissident times, even in such a chopped version, it was certainly too fragmentary to support me in America.

Learning English was hard for me – mostly because I was constantly aware that English was not Russian. I had to give up speaking my chosen language in order to speak a conglomeration of sounds that neither pleased my ears nor brought comfort to my body. But since I was in the United States by my own choice, I had no basis to complain. I had to learn English whether I liked it or not. My fellow immigrants were learning it, but very slowly. They took classes and struggled with grammar. They tried hard. Yet their English sounded as if it had been hammered out in Siberia, clumsy and heavy. It was an English I dreaded to be caught with.

I was told that a good way to learn a new language was to acquire a boyfriend who spoke it, but I was married to a Russian man at the time, and my monogamous philosophy restrained me from following that path. I needed a third way: a way in which I could learn English fast. A way that would hammer my language into a shape that would seem, if not handsome, then at least familiar to Americans, an easy fit into the English they were used to.

First, I acquired an emotion that put me at peace with the need to learn English. The emotion was compassion for the English language. I knew English would never become to me what Russian was, but I thought, "Poor you; you'll never be as dear to me as my chosen language; but that's okay: I'll learn you." I devised a system of learning English that suited me. I taught myself English, and soon I was far ahead of my immigrant friends in using the language, even though it was bound to be my step-language. So I concluded that I could teach English as a step-language to Billy. I knew how to teach a step-language. My language training had three major parts:

1. Kill the fear of language.

2. Life is emotions. A language without emotions is a lifeless language. Learn to act out emotions in a new language.

3. People speak a mundane and simple language, relying, in their daily occupations, on a perennial core of words. Know your core language.

Kill the fear of language

I don't remember how old I was before I learned that people could sound smart or sound stupid, and that one is better than the other. I learned my Russian before I knew that I might sound stupid. When the time came to learn English though, my fear of sounding stupid was already well developed. It was the same with many of my friends, some with doctorates in sciences like physics and mathematics. We used to look with envy at American children, as young three or four, rattling off English as if there was nothing to it.

I knew for sure that a fear, in whatever form, is not a friend. At different times in my life I've parted with many a fear, and this one, the fear of sounding stupid in English, had to go as well. For a long time I pondered how to do away with it, and then one day the answer came. Actually, it was one night, because I saw the answer in a dream. In that dream I was a news anchor on American television, dressed in a double-breasted suit and broadcasting – confident and self-assured – in breathtaking English.

I got up, took the newspaper, chose a small article on local politics and read it with the anchor-like intonation from my dream. My first reading seemed ridiculously far from what I intended, but by the time I had read it ten times, I sounded almost as good as I had sounded in that dream of mine, or at least I thought so.

Then I thought, if I can sound like a television news anchor, why not try to sound like an opera singer or Sean Connery? I tried to sing a passage as I imagined Luciano Pavarotti would have sung it. Again, I did it ten times. It would be a stretch to say that after ten repetitions I came close to Luciano. But the process of adjusting my operatic talent to English was, in itself, so idiotic that in the end I could not help but laugh at myself. Suddenly I realized that I was not afraid of that piece of English in front of me. The laughter killed my fear. They don't make good roommates, laughter and fear. It's one or the other. That's how I got the idea: I needed to *impersonate* English, and impersonate it in a way that would amuse me. When I learned English with that amusement in my heart, the process would dispense with my fear of getting it wrong, then I would have learned fearless English.

I chose small English texts and read them over and over, applying any voice that thrilled me at the time. I read like David Letterman. I read like the Pope. I read like President Reagan, and like Margaret Thatcher. I read like Elizabeth Taylor, like Peter Jennings, like Mao Tze Tung, and like Meryl Streep. Because I have a soft spot for preaching, my English was most satisfying when proclaimed in the voices of Billy Graham or Jimmy Swaggart.

Gradually, the fear of sounding stupid left me. In the company of Americans, I spoke what I could, surprising my Russian friends with the speed with which I spoke English – an English full of grammatical mistakes and mismatched words, to be sure, but one that got the message across without punishing the listener with the agonizing wait that accompanies constant self-judgment. I lost the need to apologize for my mistakes without losing my drive to improve my language.

Was it possible that Billy was afraid of English? He must have been, I thought, if, indeed, English was a step-language to him. He started speaking only when he was four, in Theresa's class. Maybe there was a part of him that was aware that he was not good at it. Maybe his desire to speak conflicted with his many failed attempts to speak? If so many venerable adults have a hard time acknowledging their inner fears, how could I expect a little autistic boy to acknowledge his?

From then on, in our Aristotle School, we started learning English as a step-language. The first step was to kill the fear of it; and so I began to invent ways in which Billy could manipulate English with amusement. Every new or difficult word we repeated in sets of five times, counting them on our fingers. We worked with words like "addition" and "subtraction," "dangerous" and "necessary."

I introduced Billy to the notions of "opera voice," "whisper voice," "serious voice" and "jolly voice." With this little repertoire, we said "addition" five times, then we sang "addition" five times, then we did "opera voice addition" and "whisper voice addition," until I felt that Billy could say the word without thinking, that the word was coming from his gut rather then his head.

It was amazing to see that Billy's reaction to this exercise was the same as mine had been years before. The more we acted out a new word, the more freedom I could see in Billy. I could feel him become amazed and amused at his own ability to say a word which, just a short while ago, seemed so difficult. "I can do it, Mom! I can do it! I'm smart now! I'm a genius!" Sometimes Billy needed to hug me, and I felt gratitude in his arms. Maybe it was gratitude for helping him overcome a step-language, or maybe it also was gratitude for overcoming a fear – the fear of sounding stupid.

Wanted: live drama

When we learn a native language, we learn from live people living real lives. The words that settle in our brains are freighted with the memories of the people from whom we learned the words and the circumstances in which we learned them. Some words are light, carrying few associations. Other words are heavy, loaded with memories and emotions.

When I say the word *poyezd* (train in Russian), I'm not just naming a particular machine used for transportation; I'm reviving, in a subconscious flash, the visions of my train trips from Moscow to the south and back, watching the terrain change from the severe forests of Russia to the inviting orchards of Ukraine. I see visions of railroad stations with gypsy women in large layered skirts, with children holding on to them like permanent attachments. When I say *poyezd*, I experience an old sinking sensation in the pit of my stomach, just as if I were again watching from afar an old gypsy woman telling a fortune from a trembling palm. Ever so hesitant of having my own fortune told, I just quietly wonder from afar about my fate.

When I say *kukhnya* (kitchen), I say a word so heavy with memories and emotions that I struggle not to be overwhelmed by it. But there it is, with the word, the memory of running in the freezing Moscow of mid-January and finally reaching the apartment of a friend, my fingers and my toes numb from the cold. There is the memory of being summoned to the *kukhnya* and being offered a full cup of hot tea. With the word comes the pleasure of watching the snowy cold, like a surrendered foe, from the safety of the *kukhnya*, feeling the warm tea melt the numbness from my limbs – and the conversations, the endless *kukhnya* conversations.

After fear, the main bar to learning a step-language is the lack of associations. When I had to learn the language of my new home in the United States, I did what any good student would do first: I acquired some good books and dictionaries. Learning a step-language happens most often within the boundaries of a desk. We learn that certain sounds, said together, name a certain thing. "Train" is an English word that stands for a piece of machinery used for transportation. "Kitchen" stands for a space in a building where food is cooked. "Sorrow" means an emotion which one displays at a time of great loss. "Delight" is the emotion experienced when one is pleased.

After about two months of desk-learning, I was fed up with it. I was trying to memorize words that, without lively associations attached to them, seemed dead. I was learning a depressing, shallow language. When I spoke my new English, my words were so light, so deprived of associations, that I felt that the language was flat, and that by speaking it, somehow, I became flat myself. I needed to fix that. I needed to be a part of something alive, I needed to witness live people doing live things. I needed to witness "sorrow" and "delight," not just learn their definitions.

The solution came to me one day as I was watching television. Ever so aware of how little I understood the language of the tube, I was changing channels when I stumbled upon a program which, surprisingly, seemed very understandable. It was the soap opera *All My Children*. I sat down to watch it. I watched to the end of the program. I watched the next day. I became a devoted viewer. Not that I didn't appreciate the artistic merits of the program: they were evident even to a viewer with English as handicapped as mine was then. But there was no livelier scene, at the time, that I could witness on a daily basis. *All My Children* acquainted me with a group of Americans who let me watch them and become used to their facial expressions and the gestures that accompanied their words. *All My Children* became my surrogate family. I was eavesdropping on the family members, peering through the screen into their bedrooms, listening to their secrets and witnessing their ups and downs.

Needless to say, *All My Children*, craftfully orchestrated though it was, was not a patch on the drama of Russian daily life. Still, the script tried to keep me curious and in suspense. After all, English was my step-language, and for a step-language, I thought, even a soap opera background should do. *All My Children* was a perfect teacher. All the tragic elements – broken hearts and broken marriages, augmented lies and dramatic revelations – were squeezed into amazingly simple English, an English that I was capable of learning. I was not entirely satisfied with the quality of some of the associations that I was using to store my new words, but when learning a language any associations are better than no associations at all. Many expressions from the soap have deepened my English and given it volume:

- "Why are you doing this to me?"
- "We need to talk about our relationship!"
- "How could you?"

Three months into my English studies, I found my first job in America. I was hired as an assistant accountant. I got the job thanks to some accounting courses I had taken back in my university days, to the charitable attitude of my future boss, and to my *All-my-children* English.

I've discussed learning through the five senses. Some of us insist we have a sixth one, intuition, and I claim a seventh. I can sense the weight of the associations behind the words people speak. I recognize a shallow language, one that carries few emotions attached to it, one that wasn't acquired at weddings or in cemeteries, nor listening to sweet lullabies or to parents fighting. Much of American English sounds like that to me: shallow. It's the English of many an immigrant, learned at a desk or while fighting sleep in a language class. It's a survival language, a language learned by a sheer effort, matching certain sounds with certain meanings. It's a step-language.

There is nothing wrong with that. Those who use it are grateful to know if not a beautiful English, at least enough to get by. In the evening when they go home, they can speak a chosen language. Whether it's Russian or Chinese, Spanish or Urdu, it fills their souls with memories, with visions and voices that put them in touch with ancestors, with the past, and with Earth itself.

Billy, spending most of his time within the confines of his inner world, was blocking himself from observing life around him and therefore from attaching associations to English words. When we started the Aristotle School, Billy was six. He had been speaking for about two years by then, but his vocabulary was limited. It consisted mostly of words which related to his daily needs and to dragon stories. He was also well behind his age level in all academic subjects. I knew I needed to teach him new words, and a lot of them.

We started by learning words from books; but it was not long before my seventh sense whispered to me that I was teaching a desk language. I was "explaining" new words rather then "living" new words with him. What could I do? For me, watching *All My Children* had supplied weight to the language; but that wouldn't work for Billy. It'd be like force-feeding him smoked fish.

I decided to stage little dramas in the classroom – tragedies and comedies alike. I remembered the one brief time when there had been a drastic improvement in Billy's vocabulary. It was when Theresa staged dramas in her class – *Eensy-Beensy Spider*, and, after that, *The Three Little Pigs*. Billy had a part in both plays, and he came home enchanted, eager to say his part over and over: "Not by the hair of my chinny-chin-chin!"

I've never been much of an actor. Acting requires a certain lightness of spirit, an ability to shift between different emotional spaces. I was raised in a family of very serious people, people who never shifted from their serious emotional space and for whom even the thought of doing such a thing was shameful. In my family, laughing at oneself was not the practice. I grew up not knowing that people could make fun of each other and get away with it. Could I possibly overcome this purity of my upbringing?

I began going back to Theresa's classroom to observe her circle time, to see her in action, a director and an actor at the same time in some of the most powerful stage productions I've ever seen. The other actors were three- to four-year-olds, mostly autistic, some severely autistic. From somewhere, from an invisible place, Theresa drew a magical energy which allowed her to go through her shows with patience and joy.

I had to discover a source of such energy for myself. I wished I could find a magic box with an endless supply of it. But as it was, I could only resort to training myself. I think that I could have benefited from acting classes, if only I had time for them, but I didn't. So I proceeded to construct my histrionic talents on my own.

Little by little I started staging my teaching. When Billy was learning to tell the time, we played the parts of the hour hand and the minute hand. One moved very slowly, while the other ran joyful circles in our small classroom.

Addition and subtraction I taught at imagined parties where pizza and cakes were served. There were imaginary friends with whom Billy shared his treats generously.

"OK. Your pizza has twelve pieces. How many would you like to give to Julia? Three pieces? Oh, Billy, thank you very much! That is so kind of you! How many pieces do you have left? Nine?! Wow! You still have a lot! Can you eat nine pieces all by yourself? No? Then how about, if, out of the sweetness of your heart, you share some of those pieces with Penelope?" And so on. Our math classes became filled with dilemmas which put to the test not only Billy's counting abilities, but his kindness and understanding as well.

Later, we moved on to talk about the hardships of the man who has to feed the seals at Sea World. If they're all healthy and well, they may all eat the same number of fishes. But what if some are undernourished, or don't feel well? Poor seals! Poor man! He has to add up all the fishes, seal by seal! He could certainly use some help. Billy to the rescue!

It was easy to dramatize our reading classes. The stories that I chose supplied a ready plot. I only had to make sure that my participation in it was sufficiently dramatic.

It was harder to dramatize grammar, the short and long vowels, and with the rules for capitalization. It helped to say, "Who could possibly know as many as five, and I said *five*, words with short vowel 'a' in them? It's such a hard task, I can not imagine who could name so many words for me!"

"I could!" Billy sprang from his chair, ready to surprise me. And he did name five words with short "a," and I did act immensely surprised and pleased. And then we moved to words with short "i" and short "o."

While Billy never lost his tendency to resist learning any new thing, we had finally found a recipe for altering his reactions. When new concepts were dramatized, his resistance diminished substantially. He began to be a fine student, as long as I kept alive a sense of wonder in the class, as long as I brought mysteries and enigmas into teaching.

We started our school in October. By February I finally became somewhat comfortable in cutting through the seriousness of my upbringing. Once in a while, caught up in our little school dramas, I'd forget about it altogether. One day in February, after a class, Billy raised his eyes to me and said in a quiet voice, "You're a good teacher now, Mama."

Develop your core language

Sitting on a plastic chair in the middle of a mall in San Diego, impatient, I was searching the crowd for the sight of my husband, who was to find me in that place. There was a man next to me, so relaxed he seemed dormant. Suddenly I was startled when the man began to talk loudly to himself. I eventually realized that a cellphone headset clung to the other side of his head, where I hadn't seen it, which was some evidence, at least, that he in fact may have been talking to someone else. Oblivious to my displeasure with the amount of auditory input I was receiving from his discourse, he carried on his side of the conversation.

"Hi, honey. Yep. It's me. What's up? Nothing much? Yep. That's how it goes. No kidding! I'll be darned! Nah. Not me. Did she? That's disgusting! Yep. I've got the shoes. Yep. Cool! You can say that again. Really cool! Who said? Tell 'em to bug off. It's a free country. No kidding. So, what else? Nothing much? That's how it goes. OK, honey. So long. Keep in touch. Sure. Nah! I'll be there. My treat. Yep. Love you. Yep. By. Yep."

By the last "yep," I spotted my husband's tall frame measuring slow steps toward the sitting area. I jumped up, freeing myself from the plastic feeling of the chair and the plastic feeling of the conversation I'd overheard. I couldn't help but wrinkle my nose at the language my accidental neighbor had used. It was so impoverished, so barren. For some time after that, my thoughts kept returning to the incident; and eventually it came to me that I had actually had the good fortune to witness an admirable concoction of English words, a model that, used properly, could ensure successful participation in practically any conversation.

"Sure. Cool. Say it again. Keep in touch." Those words and phrases were a core. One could add a little here, a little there. But the core was a group of words which one could say without thinking and which could be perceived without thinking. I realized that while I had this sort of core language in Russian and Romanian, I have never developed one in English. I did not have even a handful of words that I could use as automatically as the ones the man in the mall used. In English, I had to choose every word, I had to construct every single sentence from zero. No wonder I had failed to experience any gratification in English-language gossip, while I could certainly relish gossip in Russian.

I also realized that Billy, like me, had no core language. He was much slower than typical children to react verbally in any situation. Maybe he pushed people so often – his sister and others – because he didn't know how to make his intentions known with words. But if he were ever to react with words, he had to have a core of them, an array which he could choose from automatically wherever he might find himself.

So we started working on a core of English, both for Billy and for me. The first step was to choose the core words, then to single out three or four at a time and to use those words consistently myself in any situation in which they seemed appropriate. I also needed to coax Billy into using them as often as I did, until we could come to a point where the words would pour out of us automatically, rather than our having to seek them and drag them out. Then we would go after another set of words until they, in their turn, flowed naturally from us.

Our first set of words was "sure", "really", and "good idea". The second set was "not again", "yes, Mama", and "wait a minute". We worked on "impossible", "let's see", "not really", "of course", "you know", "not much", "another time", "no way", "disgusting", "sweet dreams", "and so", and "once upon a time". Some of our core language was inspired by the man in the mall – "cool", "nothing much", and "no kidding".

We worked on those all that year. The next we moved on to a more elaborate core language. We worked on "naturally", "that's too hard", "may I", "grateful", and "not a good idea". Being naturally dramatic, Billy developed an affinity for such words as "preposterous" and "breathtaking". He makes big eyes when says those. Billy took wonderfully well to training his core language. He loves letting new words grow into him. Sometimes the training has taken an unexpected turn. Billy's overuse of "disgusting" at the dinner table called for a substitution. We went for "It does not speak to me" – as in, "This fish does not speak to me, Mama."

Here and there I've noticed Billy make innovative additions to his core language – like "I'll hit you on your head", "I'll punch your nose", or "Na-na-na-na-na-na" accompanied by two hands flapping at his ears. With these I had to work in reverse, i.e., to eradicate them. But I couldn't help being secretly pleased with his using those expressions. In the old times, he would have hit or punched someone. Now he merely talks about it.

The core language helped Billy with his social interactions. Before, he tended to touch children as a way to establish contact. Most children do not like to be touched, especially when the touch is likely to be a squeeze or a punch. With some core language at hand, Billy began to contact children verbally.

Billy also became a storyteller. He designs his stories as he tells them. While in the process of developing yet another dragon tale, he stays in touch with his audience, thanks to "you know", "and so", or "sure enough". And I'm making progress with my own core language in English. My favorites are "I beg your pardon", "This is tragic", "I shall not tolerate such a thing", "by God's will", "You think you're Romeo and I'm Juliet?" and "Let's not use superlative words for mediocre feelings".

Overall, Billy's English has improved tremendously. His happy wordplay is quite magical. The best of the magic, though, is not so much in Billy's juggling so many words at once as in his conceiving the mystery of the language. I can see that, more and more, he sees words as precious stones and himself as a craftsman who can use those stones to create a masterpiece. He is even up to venturing into unknown languages.

"Mom, I think I remember how dragons speak. You know, dragons have a language."

"Really?"

"Yes. Do you want me to teach you?"

"Sure, Billy. Teach me the dragon language."

"Well, 'Hachi' means 'hi' in the dragon language. 'Taro' means 'danger'. 'Tochaka' means 'fight'."

"Billy, it sounds like the dragon language is beautiful."

"Yes, Mom, it's really beautiful. Maybe I could write a book when I grow up and teach people the dragon language?"

"Of course you can. I think it will be wonderful to know the dragon language. That means we could learn to speak to dragons."

"So, Mom, you really believe that dragons are real?"

"Yes, I do. I think they are as real as you and me."

"Oh, Mom, it would be so wonderful to have mighty dragons for friends!"

But before we have mighty dragons for friends, we're making friends with words of the mighty English language, and it will be a long-lasting, wonderful friendship. No kidding.

dragon
fiery breath
eats slow people
dragons burn ihme
burn

Chapter 19

Every person has a story

- A typical child starts practicing talking to other children at an early age.

- Billy, at six years of age, lacked the skill of verbal interaction with his peers.

- My task: to teach Billy to approach people verbally.

Billy didn't have friends of his own until the spring of his second grade. Before that, his major interaction with children was with his sister, and with Julia and Penelope, the daughters of our close friends. These three girls had known him for a long time and were trained in handling Billy's autistic traits.

At school, though, the children didn't think of Billy as fun to play with. Actually, they avoided him; they turned down his requests to play. It was hard to blame them. For a start, Billy didn't talk with them. He didn't know the rules for games. When someone tried to explain the rules to him, he didn't want to listen; or if he listened, he didn't want to follow the rules, he came up with rules of his own. He was impulsive, both emotionally and physically. When things weren't to Billy's liking, he tended to be aggressive; sometimes he punched or pushed.

That's why I went with him to the field at school. I followed him closely to be ready to prevent him from having a tantrum or from hurting someone. It was after my discovery of Billy's inability to connect the world around him that I thought that he might not have any idea how to approach other children. What were they to Billy? How were they different from a ball? From a dragon? And so we did a Net Fixer.

Every person has a story

Mom: Billy, why are you so rough with the children on the field?

Billy: Because. I want to play tag. And if they don't, I get mad.

Mom: What if they want to play another game?

Billy: I don't want to play another game.

Mom: I understand. You want to play tag. Can you play tag with a tree?

Billy: No, Mom. Trees don't play tag.

Mom: Right. It's because they are not alive, right?

Billy: Right.

Mom: But all the children are alive. They have names. How come you forget to ask the children their names before you play?

Billy: I don't know.

Mom: Do you like it when people remember your name?

Billy: Yes.

Mom: Well, the other children like it too. You see, Billy, every person has a story. But all our stories are different.

Billy: How?

Mom: Well, I have a mother. Do I have the same mother as you do?

Billy: No.

Mom: Do Julia and Penelope have the same mother as you do?

Billy: No.

Mom: Do they live in the same house as you do?

Billy: No. They have their own house.

Mom: Does Julia like to play the same games as you do?

Billy: No. She likes to play dolls.

Mom: Right. You see, every child has a different story. He has a mom of his own and a dad of his own. He has a place where he lives, a bed where he sleeps. He has his own toys to play with. Every child has special toys.

Billy: Like my dragons?

Mom: Yes, like your dragons. Every child likes some special books or TV shows. What is your special TV show?

Billy: *Dragonland!*

Mom: And every child has a special movie. What is your special movie?

Billy: *Star Wars.*

Mom: Now, when you go to school, on the field you will meet many children. Before you ask someone to play with you, first you need to ask them about their story.

Billy: I don't know how.

Mom: I will help you. First, you will ask them their *name.* Then you could ask any question about their story. You can ask about their toys, about their house, about their books, about their movies. Would you try?

Billy: Okay, I'll try.

Mom: Billy, that is how people start when they go about making new friends. They start with asking about the person's story.

We made a drawing to go with the Net Fixer (shown opposite).

The story made sense to Billy. That day when we went to the school, I spotted a boy whom I knew a little. I knew that he was one of the more tolerant children. I told Billy to go to him and to ask him about his story. "Start by asking his name, then ask about movies or TV shows," I prompted him.

Billy did as I suggested, except that he started not by asking the boy's name, but by asking, "What's your story?" I jumped in: "No, no, Billy. First of all, 'What's your name?'"

To my delight, Billy did end up talking to the boy. They walked, for a while, in a field full of noise and commotion that children make when they're freed from their classrooms. As I followed at a respectful distance, I could hear Billy talking excitedly about *Star Wars* and about his dragons. The other boy spoke too quietly for me to hear him, but he actually managed to get in some words in return.

Mystery me   Billy Holland

I was born in Mount Pleasants in New York state, on August 31 1993.

Baby Billy

I'm good at pictures of dragons and dinos I'm also good at reading adventure books.

All about Me

I love to be gentle. I also love to snuggle quietly in my bed.

I hate being alone. I hate eating fish and rice.

My favourite show is Batman Because it has action.

My favourite Book is Boffalo Women Because it has beautiful pictures

This incident didn't change our lives in any drastic way. Lacking my prompting, Billy would still be lifted by the energy of the field into wild and loud play. But here and there, when I'd remind him to ask a child his story, Billy would stop and actually find the child's face and say, "What's your name? My name is Billy."

Then toward the end of second grade, Billy made his first friend. The other boy also had some social difficulties, and Billy became his first friend as well. At some point they started seeking each other on the field. They began to walk and talk together. I suppose they shared their stories.

The Fox

There once was a fox
who sat on a box.

People who passed him
had pies thrown at them.

They didn't like pie,
so they said goodbye.

Billy

PART IV

Afterthoughts and Milestones

The Sun

The sun rose day by day;
the shadows went away;

from the sky he saw a hen;
then he went down again.

When he rose again, he said hello to the hen;
I'm going to write a letter with my pen,
said the hen.

Billy

Chapter 20

In search of humor

Webster's dictionary tells us that humor is, among other things, "the mental faculty of discovering, expressing or appreciating ludicrous or absurdly incongruous elements." I've been told that my mother-in-law, who left for a better world before I married her son, had this mental faculty. We see traces of that faculty in some of her grandchildren.

Some of humankind have a faculty that allows them to appreciate music. Others have to undergo hours of training with a music teacher to achieve the same appreciation. We learn to train many faculties in ourselves that do not come naturally to us. But we do not have teachers of humor, teachers who would come to our children and conduct classes that train "the mental faculty of discovering, expressing or appreciating ludicrous or absurdly incongruous elements." I've wished often and deeply that there were such teachers. I'd sign up for a class. I'd take my children with me.

In my family, we didn't joke. I have a faint memory of myself, very small, liking to hear myself laugh, but I was taught to let go of that liking. My parents didn't know how to joke. My grandparents didn't know how to joke either. Of course, life in times of war, of communist rule and other hardships wasn't conducive to the development of a faculty for humor. Instead, we knew how to be serious. We knew how to be sad and how to take pride in our sadness.

In principle, there is nothing wrong with living a serious life. Life goes on even when it's serious. There are serious jobs in the world. A serious job can pay the bills. But in the job of parenting a child, being serious is a limitation. Because children like to hear themselves laugh, and it's quite wonderful to let them do that. It's even better to inspire their laughter.

In our Aristotle School, as I taught Billy to read and write, I taught myself about humor. My first attempts at flexing my mental faculty to create something absurdly incongruous were absurdly incongruous. But I went on from there. The reason for my effort was simple. I noticed that it was easier to teach a smiling Billy than a serious Billy. We could endure a far longer journey into knowledge on a smile than on a serious mood. I needed to learn how to create smiles.

My training came by trial and error. I'd try something and observe Billy's reaction. If he was amused, than I'd succeeded in creating something humorous. If he wasn't, I hadn't. It was as simple as that. I tried many things. Billy thinks it absurdly incongruous when I spread five of my fingers on top of my head and announce that I'm the Queen of England. I've learned to make ludicrous faces, to pretend that I stammer, to roll my eyes dramatically, to sing in an operatic manner (truly ludicrous, with my voice). Anything to get a smile.

My children's smiles look to me like rainbows. Their smiles make them light and clean. They shine, just as the world shines after rain. It took me a while to realize that when I smile, they see me in the same way. They see a rainbow.

Alliteration

Billy Bopp
had a fine feathered friend.
His friend was a heavenly hockey-playing hen.
For lunch they ate a two-ton tomato
and delicious dessert
including icy icky ice cream.
For dinner they dined
on a purple potato.
Then they danced the jigger-bug jig.
They went to bed
with two-tone teddies
and slept like a big balloon butterfly.

Chapter 21

Why Aristotle?

Indeed, why Aristotle? Every endeavor needs an inspiration. I needed an inspiration when I embarked on teaching Billy. Aristotle as an inspiration was as good as any could be. Not that I can call myself a scholar of his philosophical legacy, not even close. About Aristotle I knew only the basics: that he stood at the beginning of modern science; that he outlined the future for many sciences – physics, logic, biology, medicine; that his approach was wonderfully inconsistent, by present-day standards. On one hand, he was the first to create theories of the need for scientific proof, i.e., controlled experiments to substantiate ideas. On the other hand, he was an ardent believer in metaphysics, comfortable with otherworldly concepts – such as spirits, the soul and God – with which no one has conducted controlled experiments, not only in his time, but still more than two thousand years later.

Aristotle's greatness, his striving to encompass all that was known at the time, is striking. His effort to connect all the sciences, to find a common spiritual denominator in everything material, is awe-inspiring to me. The images of him that we have inherited show a robust man, very handsome in an intelligent sort of way – definitely not a nerd. For all his learning, he looks as physical as if he unloaded ships for a living. I took that as an inspiration as well.

Aristotle managed to produce a vast body of highly acclaimed work. One would have thought that the man would have had little time left to be bothered with happiness. With such a brain as his, who needs happiness? And yet he sought after it. Happiness was important to Aristotle. I needed that for an inspiration, very much so. I was brought up in an ideology that called us to sacrifice our happiness for the happiness of future generations. Our ideology gave no exact guidance as to which generation, finally, would get to be happy. Not to be happy was the norm. When I lived in the Soviet Union, I was sharply sensitive to some of the deprivations – of freedom, of books, of ideas. The deprivation of happiness didn't bother me.

Later, when I had my children, I came to resent my acquiescence in non-happiness. I suddenly wanted happiness, and plenty of it. And not only for future generations. I wanted happiness for myself, for my own generation. Thus, Aristotle became my inspiration. I kept him as my beacon when I reasoned that, since there was no guidance on coping with autism, I might as well use all the world around me to teach me how to deal with Billy's autism. Aristotle had tried to connect all the world around him. I would too, for Billy.

From Chinese medicine I've learned to perform accupressure on Billy. Massaging, applying light pressure, on his fingertips and on the sides of his fingernails, calms him wonderfully, and I could do it anytime, anywhere.

From Quentin Tarantino I've learned not to see the television set as only a "box for the stupid." For Quentin, who, as I understand, was raised by a single mother, the "box" was a baby-sitter and an educator which tutored him in the subject of film-making.

From Ronald Reagan I've learned to use superlative expressions when the times require them. Oh, how right he was, calling the USSR "an evil empire!"

From trees, which know when to drop their leaves, I've learned to let go of yesterday's troubles. Tomorrow, surely, will have troubles of its own.

From Donna Eden's energy therapy book *Energy Medicine* I've learned to tap on energy points of my body or the bodies of my children. Whether to calm down hyperactivity or to dispel a nightmare, it has brought wonderful results.

From my nanny I've learned to ignore an unfriendly back.

From the moon I've learned that one doesn't have to be a wolf to be made to howl.

From the sun I've learned about unasked giving.

From hypnotherapy I've learned the ways of the subconscious mind.

From the movie *My Big Fat Greek Wedding* I've gained support for my approach to language training.

From Liz Taylor I've learned that there's always another chance.

From Gurdjiev I've learned discipline.

From Shakespeare I've learned that the world is a stage and all of us are poor players on it. From him, as well, I've learned to ask myself whether to be or not to be.

From the Communists I've learned how to insure that an endeavor would fail.

From computer programming I've learned that I could fit my thinking into the blocks of a flow chart.

From algebra I've learned that if I put together my brains and my efforts, they will equal a result. And that the reverse, putting together my efforts and my brains, works exactly the same way. If I have more than zero in my brains and more than zero in my efforts, the result would be more than zero, as well.

From Billy, I'm still learning.

Chapter 22

Milestones

October 23, 2000

Dictation.

the sun is up.

the boy is big.

the boy has a hat.

the hat is red.

These were the milestones of Billy's journey in the Aristotle School.

First grade

October

- We start with repeating the alphabet and simple addition. We learn to distinguish odd and even numbers.

November

- We learn the short vowels.
- We start reading from a second grade reading book. It's slow going. We read every story three times: I read it to him; he reads it to me to get the words; and then he reads it again to me for speed. Billy loves the progress.
- We start simple subtraction.

December

- Reading is more of the same, plus we work on memorizing poems.
- Comparing numbers and identifying which is larger.

January

- We try to work on money and time; but they are too hard. Addition and subtraction, though, go very well, and we move into simple regrouping.
- We're about to be finished with the short vowels. We do well with compound words, synonyms and antonyms.

February

- We start long vowels.
- We return to clocks and time, and this time Billy has more understanding.
- Reading the second grade book becomes easier and easier.

March

- We continue long vowels, and for arithmetic we start regrouping in addition and subtraction. We introduce measurements.

April

- We work a lot on word examples to illustrate short and long vowels. We learn about nouns and verbs.
- We come back to money and time.

May

- Billy is very good at first grade math, except money and time, which are still problems.
- His writing is not tidy, but he reads very well.

Second grade

September

- Back in school, we quickly review first grade math. Billy remembers it well. We go over money and time, and this time his understanding of it is better.

- He remembers all he learned in our language classes.

- Loma Portal Elementary tests Billy on all subjects. On tests given to typical students, he tests at his age or above.

October

- We study common and proper nouns and rules for capitalization. We read from a third grade reading book.

- We start multiplication.

November

- We memorize multiplication by one, two and three. I start dictating passages for Billy to write.

December

- Billy learns to multiply by four. Our addition and subtraction moves into hundreds.

January

- Multiplication by five.

- We start reading from a fifth grade reading book, jumping the fourth grade. It's hard and slow, but we both enjoy the progress and working with new words. Billy's vocabulary increases substantially.

February

- Multiplication by six.

- Billy does well in English. We work on definitions for nouns and verbs, and learn about proper and common nouns.

March

- Multiplication by seven. We do graphs. More measurements. Identifying large numbers and distinguishing which is greater.

April

- Multiplication by eight. Fractions.
- Adjectives.

Billy takes the GATE test. The GATE ("Gifted and Talented Education") test is given to students in the San Diego school system in second grade to identify students who may qualify for special courses or classes for gifted students. Students who do very well qualify for advanced classes ("GATE classes").

Students who do extraordinarily well (99.9 percentile, i.e., one out of a thousand; or for students with certain learning disabilities, including autism, 99.6 percentile, i.e., four out of a thousand) qualify for a special class: "Seminar." Seminar classes are organized in many schools throughout the San Diego school system, and a student who qualifies can enroll in any of them, instead of in his local school (subject to an allocation system if some schools are over subscribed).

The GATE test uses an intelligence test known as the Raven Matrices, after Mr. Raven, who devised them. The Raven Matrices are a set of problems requiring identification of analogies between shapes. They are designed to be culture-neutral, and may even be language-neutral.

From early in his life, Billy has shown that he has an architectural mind. He builds things – from boxes, from sticks, from paper and tape. He doesn't just build things, he designs things to build. To a boy with language problems, the Raven Matrices are freedom. They are his open field. We want Billy to take the GATE test. The teacher of his inclusion class does not want him to take the GATE test along with his class. She is afraid he will disturb the typical children. This is not an unfounded fear. Billy, distracted, can be a distraction.

We work to arrange for Billy to take the GATE test separately. The test is given throughout the district by one school psychologist, a Chinese gentleman. My husband has numerous telephone discussions with him, trying to work out a schedule when he can make a special trip to Loma Portal so one boy can take the test alone. The Chinese gentleman is accommodating, but his schedule is busy. We also want Billy to have his aide in the room for the test, not for assistance (which isn't allowed), but to be able to take him out of the room for a break if he needs one. The Chinese gentleman has no objection to the aide, although, he points out, he has given the GATE test by himself to plenty of children with learning disabilities. At length the schedule is worked out, although not before my husband and the Chinese gentleman become well acquainted by telephone.

The Chinese gentleman, the aide and Billy all appear in the same room at Loma Portal at the same time. Billy takes the test. He comes home with a piece of paper on which the gentleman has written his name in Chinese. Billy shows it to us proudly. How does he think he did on the test. "Oh, okay, I think."

The Chinese gentleman calls the next day. "Well, I watched the boy zip through the first set," he says, "and I thought, hmmm, well... But I had to wait until I could score the whole thing." Billy's score is 99.7. He has qualified for Seminar. The Chinese gentleman is as proud as if Billy were his own boy.

May

- Multiplication by nine.
- Adverbs.

We look at schools not too far from our home that have Seminar classes Billy might attend. He will need a full-time aide. The school district is supportive. We find a class, third and fourth grades combined, with a friendly teacher who has some ten years of experience in special education. Billy likes her; she likes him. We apply to have him attend her class. We are hopeful, but the school, Sunset View, is not our local elementary school, and kids who are local there have first preference. By the end of the school year, we have good news: Billy will be a full-time student at Sunset View's Seminar class.

The Aristotle School for the Bright and Gifted has lost its only student, but its lost student is certified bright and gifted.

Epilogue

There is a story I love. It's about an Englishman. In the 1920s, he owned a successful bookstore and enjoyed a pleasurable life. Yet a longing gnawed at his heart, although he wasn't quite sure what he longed for. One day he left the store to his partner and went to a far-away country, to a place where, on large wooded grounds, there lived a spiritual teacher and few of his disciples.

The spiritual teacher welcomed the Englishman. He took the Englishman deep into the forest, gave him a shovel and said to him: "There is a spring around here. Dig for it." The teacher left. The Englishman started digging. He dug many days, to no avail. He went through many emotions during those days. One day, he'd enjoy the physical labor, the forest and the fresh air. Another day, he'd feel utterly stupid about his digging, and he'd wonder why on earth he had left a successful business and a pleasurable life to spend his days digging the ground for nothing.

But something kept him going, whether stubbornness or something else. There came a day when he got angry. There came a day when he didn't care anymore why he was digging. And there came a day when he crashed his shovel into the earth and saw... No, he didn't see. At first, he felt the water with his bare feet. Then he saw it. The teacher was right. There was a spring in the forest.

The Englishman kept digging until he had made a comfortable channel for the water. As he touched the cool stream, he felt his longing fulfilled. Something in him was becoming complete.

That night the other disciples came to the spring, and there was a party, with singing and laughter. The teacher didn't come. It was the Englishman's party. It was his spring.

There were times in my journey of Olga-as-parent when I had to take a shovel and start digging. I was digging through the grounds of my upbringing, through the forest of my beliefs, through the stones of my illusions. The spring that I sought was hard to find. I dug for the spring of compassion, for the spring of tolerance, for the spring of silence, for the spring of laughter.

One day, after lunch, I was about to take Billy to Loma Portal Elementary for the two hours of his inclusion program. We were late and, seeing Billy playing with a stick in the yard, I rushed him to the car. "Billy, come on, hurry up. And it's not such a good idea to play with that stick. You may get... You may get... I forgot how you call that thing!"

I ran to the car, Billy with me. I was annoyed to have forgotten a seemingly simple word, but with a step-language that happens often. As I backed the car from the driveway, Billy, from his back seat, said, "Mom, Jesus will help you."

"Yeah, right," I answered, not quite sure what he meant. As we drove to the school, we passed Homer Street, then Goldsmith Street. As we approached Freeman Street, I had a flash of memory: "Splinter! I meant you could have gotten a splinter playing with that stick!"

Billy, filled with joy, clapped his hands on his knees. "See, Mom, see? I told you Jesus will help you! I told you!"

When digging for yet another stream, there may be harsh times, but the gods help. One may recognize the help, or not; but it's there.

We, the people, don't always like one another very much. When we don't like a spouse, we divorce. When we don't like a neighbor, we build a wall. When we don't like an enemy, we kill. When we don't like nations, we build iron curtains.

There's no hiding from autism. It looks at us through eyes bigger than the children to whom they belong. It's a haunting look. It will haunt a person across the face of this earth and beyond it – unless that person, longing for peace for the soul, learns to take a shovel and dig: to dig for all the streams on earth until, one day, that longing may be quenched. And then, let there be a party – one with singing and laughter.

I am Billy

I am smart and happy
I wonder if the earth will
be green
I hear birds
I see beautiful rainbows
I want freedom
I am smart and happy

I pretend to fly
I feel skins
I touch trees
I worry about many
things
I cry at dead things
I am smart and happy

I understand my Mom
I say good luck
I dream of dragons
I try working
I hope for goodness
I am smart and happy

I am Billy

Index